AF589177

JAMES BALDWIN'S "SONNY'S BLUES"

Tom Jenks's reading of James Baldwin's "Sonny's Blues" follows a scene-by-scene, sometimes line-by-line, discussion of the pattern by which Baldwin indelibly writes "Sonny's Blues" into the consciousness of readers.

It provides ongoing observations of the aesthetics underlying the particulars of the story, with references to Edward P. Jones (whose magnificent story "All Aunt Hagar's Children" bears a knowing relationship to "Sonny's Blues"), to Charlie Parker's music, and to Billie Holiday's "Am I Blue?" and John Coltrane's "A Love Supreme" as part of the musical progression Baldwin creates, and with attention to Baldwin's oratorical gifts and the biblical references in the story, to its time structure, characterizations, dramatic action, and, most of all, its totality of effect.

Drawing on Baldwin's book-length essay *The Fire Next Time*, which Baldwin published six years after the publication of the short story, Tom Jenks offers insight into some of the sources in Baldwin's life for "Sonny's Blues" and on the logic and passion by which life may be meaningfully transformed into art.

Further Praise for *James Baldwin's "Sonny's Blues"*

'It is a commonplace to think the book always wiser than the reader, but in Jenks's case the reader-critic really is on a par with the fiction. He brings a poet's eye to bear on the big-picture sweep of a fiction theorist, and there is something delightful on every page.'

Times Literary Supplement

'Tom Jenks's appreciation of Baldwin's story is almost as moving as the text itself. It's brilliant, perfectly elucidating not only Baldwin's writing, but reminding us of the unspoken agreement between writer and reader that reading can transport us most when each person brings equal passion to the task.'

Ann Beattie, author of *The New Yorker Stories*

'Jenks's reverence for the story and for Baldwin's gift with language enlivens the [...] analysis, imparting the feeling of sitting in on a favorite professor's lecture. It's an erudite testament to the pleasures of savoring a text.'

Publishers Weekly

TOM JENKS

JAMES BALDWIN'S "SONNY'S BLUES"

Great Clarendon Street, Oxford, OX2 6DP,
United Kingdom

Oxford University Press is a department of the University of Oxford. It furthers the University's objective of excellence in research, scholarship, and education by publishing worldwide. Oxford is a registered trade mark of Oxford University Press in the UK and in certain other countries.

© Tom Jenks 2024

The moral rights of the author have been asserted.

First published in 2024

First published in paperback in 2026

All rights reserved. No part of this publication may be reproduced, stored in a retrieval system, transmitted, used for text and data mining, or used for training artificial intelligence, in any form or by any means, without the prior permission in writing of Oxford University Press, or as expressly permitted by law, by licence or under terms agreed with the appropriate reprographics rights organization. Enquiries concerning reproduction outside the scope of the above should be sent to the Rights Department, Oxford University Press, at the address above.

You must not circulate this work in any other form and you must impose this same condition on any acquirer.

Links to third party websites are provided by Oxford in good faith and for information only. Oxford disclaims any responsibility for the materials contained in any third party website referenced in this work.

Published in the United States of America by Oxford University Press
546 Fifth Avenue, New York, NY 10036, United States of America

British Library Cataloguing in Publication Data
Data available

Library of Congress Control Number: 2023951736

ISBN 9780192884244 (hbk)
ISBN 9780192884268 (pbk)

DOI: 10.1093/oso/9780192884244.001.0001

The manufacturer's authorized representative in the EU for product safety is Oxford University Press España S.A. of Parque Empresarial San Fernando de Henares, Avenida de Castilla, 2 – 28830 Madrid (www.oup.es/en or product.safety@oup.com). OUP España S.A. also acts as importer into Spain of products made by the manufacturer.

My Reading

SERIES INTRODUCTION

This series is built on a simple presupposition: that it helps to have a book recommended and discussed by someone who cares for it. Books are not purely self-sufficient: they need people and they need to get to what is personal within them.

The people we have been seeking as contributors to *My Reading* are readers who are also writers: novelists and poets; literary critics, outside as well as inside universities, but also thinkers from other disciplines—philosophy, psychology, science, theology, and sociology—beside the literary; and, not least of all, intense readers whose first profession is not writing itself but, for example, medicine, or law, or a nonverbal form of art. Of all of them we have asked: what books or authors feel as though they are deeply *yours*, influencing or challenging your life and work, most deserving of rescue and attention, or demanding of feeling and use?

What is it like to love this book? What is it like to have a thought or idea or doubt or memory, not cold and in abstract, but live in the very act of reading? What is it like to feel, long after, that this writer is a vital part of your life? We ask our authors to respond to such bold questions by writing not conventionally but personally—whatever "personal" might mean, whatever form or style it might take, for them as individuals. This does not mean overt confession at the expense of a chosen book or author; but nor should our writers be afraid of making autobiographical connections. What was wanted was whatever made for their own hardest thinking in careful relation to quoted sources and specifics. The work was to go on in the taut and resonant space between these readers and their chosen books. And the interest within that area begins precisely when it is no longer clear how much is coming from the text and how much is coming from its readers—where that distinction is no longer easily tenable because neither is sacrificed to the other. That would show what reading meant at its most serious and how it might have relation to an individual life.

Out of what we hope will be an ongoing variety of books and readers, *My Reading* offers personal models of what it is like to care about particular authors, to re-create through specific examples imaginative versions of what those authors and works represent, and to show their effect upon a reader's own thinking and development.

ANNE CHENG
PHILIP DAVIS
JACQUELINE NORTON
MARINA WARNER
MICHAEL WOOD

For my children and their children, and for future generations.
We are all just people here.

CONTENTS

PROLOGUE

Growing up white in middle-class Northern Virginia in the 1950s and '60s, a couple of hours away from the capital of the Confederacy, I floated unconsciously within a racist culture. My maternal grandparents lived in Montgomery, Alabama, and visiting them as a small boy, I became aware of George Wallace during his first gubernatorial race—one he would lose because he hadn't taken a hard enough segregationist line—but I knew nothing about Wallace except his campaign photographs and the charge of excitement, or frisson, attending him in the quiet backyard twilight greenness of the neighborhood where my grandparents and their friends sat in lawn chairs and talked over their days while the children lazed about. Much later, I attended a Southern boarding school that dated from before the Civil War. The school depended on a resident staff of workers who lived in a building that also housed the coal-fired heating plant and that was known as "Black McGuire," there being another building, a student dormitory, named "McGuire" after an early headmaster who oversaw the closing of the school during the Civil War. From time to time, during my years at the school, an illustrious old boy, such as Virginius Dabney, a descendant of Thomas Jefferson and an editor of the *Richmond Times-Dispatch,* would return to the school and be given a seat at the right hand of the headmaster at dinner and afterward be asked to say some words to the assembled student body. When the old boy took the lectern, his audience of boys at their white-linen-covered dining tables began to stamp their feet and shout in unison, "Buster! Buster! Buster!" until finally after long moments an old Black man dressed in kitchen whites—the school dishwasher, who had been at his duties through generations of boys—emerged through a swinging door and bowed while the dining room erupted in an adoring applause of self-confirmation until Buster backed through the swinging door and returned to his duties. I began to feel a sorrowing discomfort that grew to alienation and then to suppressed rage at Southern white complacent privilege. The school sat on a hilltop overlooking Washington, DC, and one night in April 1968, the spring of my senior year, I sat alone on the grassy hill, watching DC burn during the riots following the assassination of Martin Luther King Jr. No one else came out of the dorms and halls to witness the wrath and despair, no one had much to say about it. Later that spring when the school announced, not by assembly but by a letter in each student's mailbox, as if such sensitive news could be communicated only privately and certainly not openly celebrated, that the following year the first Black student would enter the school—a world-beater of a student, a scholar, a star athlete—one night several burning crosses appeared on the front lawn of the main building. I'm glad to say I didn't know which of my schoolmates decided to imitate the Ku Klux Klan and sad to say that afterward nothing was said or done about it, except to remove the charred evidence as if nothing had happened. Not long ago I met a young Black woman who recently attended the school on an athletic scholarship and who confirmed what I suspected—that while some things have changed, they have not changed nearly enough.

I can't recall when I first read James Baldwin's "Sonny's Blues," but I had it well in mind in 1984 when Raymond Carver and I were selecting stories for our anthology *American Short Story Masterpieces,* the inspiration for which was an earlier anthology, *Short Story Masterpieces,* edited by Robert Penn Warren and Albert Erskine. That book was a standard text in literature and writing classes from its publication in 1954 throughout the next several decades. I'd read and loved the Penn Warren/Erskine anthology as a college student, and some years later I noticed a copy of it on a bookshelf in the guest bedroom of a professor's house in Arkansas, where I was visiting overnight to give a talk on publishing the next day. I opened the book, with a feeling of revisiting an old friend, and on the copyright page I was reminded by the publication date that the collection had been around and popular for course adoption for thirty-some years. It was time, I thought, for a new collection. Early on, when I was first at work in publishing, an editor whom I was replacing asked what I was interested in. "Masterpieces," I said with the happy confidence of youth. The more experienced editor laughed and said, "Well, you're going to collect a lot of paychecks between masterpieces." She was right of course, but masterpieces remain the most abidingly worthwhile works to read. When Ray Carver and I worked on our selections, we would meet in Manhattan, where I lived, or in Syracuse, New York, where he lived. Whichever of us had traveled brought a suitcase full of books, and the other contributed an accumulated stack. We'd trade books. Each morning we'd read and then meet for lunch and talk about what we'd read. After lunch we'd read some more, and at dinner we talked about the afternoon's reading. Sometimes we'd reread at the other's behest. Our conversations were not analytical. Typically, the recognition of a story for inclusion was an immediate, mutual response: "Wow, that's a great story! Yes!" Conversation ended there, in certainty, with a selection easily made.

Auden noted, "Pleasure is by no means an infallible critical guide, but it is the least fallible."[1] Anyone who reads professionally, as an editor, writer, teacher, agent, or publisher, becomes readily aware of the overwhelming mediocrity that attends most literary effort. Tolstoy, in his somewhat didactic but nonetheless brilliant way, observed:

> We are surrounded by productions considered artistic. Thousands of verses, thousands of poems, thousands of novels, thousands of dramas, thousands of pictures, thousands of musical pieces, follow one after another. All the verses describe love, or nature, or the author's state of mind, and in all of them rhyme and rhythm are observed. All the dramas and comedies are splendidly mounted and are performed by admirably trained actors. All the novels are divided into chapters; all of them describe love, contain effective situations, and correctly describe the details of life. All the symphonies contain *allegro, andante, scherzo,* and *finale*; all consist of modulations and chords, and are played by highly-trained musicians. All the pictures, in gold frames, saliently depict faces and sundry accessories. But among these productions in the various branches of art there is in each branch one among hundreds of thousands, not only somewhat better than the rest, but differing from them as a diamond differs from paste. The one is priceless, the others not only have no value but are worse than valueless, for they deceive and pervert taste . . .
>
> How is one to discriminate? . . .
>
> For a country peasant of unperverted taste this is as easy as it is for an animal of unspoiled scent to follow the trace he needs among a thousand others in wood or forest. The animal unerringly finds

[1] W. H. Auden, "Reading" (New York: Vintage, 1989; *Narrative*, 2008), https://www.narrativemagazine.com/issues/winter-2008/classics/reading-w-h-auden.

> what he needs. So also the man, if only his natural qualities have not been perverted, will, without fail, select from among thousands of objects the real work of art he requires—that infecting him with the feeling experienced by the artist.[2]

Amid the mediocrity—the baseline static or white noise, cliché, approximation, and shorthand—that necessarily suffuses daily life in order that the effort of communication doesn't exhaust everyone, the presence of originality, wit, authenticity, and truth announces itself like a seismographic spike to anyone receptive to the quality of accurate experience. Innately, within every reader, even a jaded, hypercritical professional reader, such as an editor or teacher burdened by mountains of manuscripts can sometimes tend to be, there is what I call an innocent reader. Eudora Welty, in her memoir *One Writer's Beginnings*, recalled that as a child when she was read to, and ever after when she read to herself, she always heard a voice:

> It isn't my mother's voice, or the voice of any person I can identify, certainly not my own. It is human, but inward, and it is inwardly that I listen to it. It is to me the voice of the story or the poem itself. The cadence, whatever it is that asks you to believe, the feeling that resides in the printed word, reaches me through the reader-voice . . .
>
> My own words, when I am at work on a story, I hear too as they go, in the same voice that I hear when I read in books. When I write and the sound of it comes back to my ears, then I act to make changes. I have always trusted this voice.[3]

[2] Leo Tolstoy, from *What Is Art?*, in *The Portable Tolstoy*, ed. John Bayley (New York: Penguin, 1978), 841–42.

[3] Eudora Welty, *One Writer's Beginnings* (Cambridge: Harvard University Press, 1984), 11–12.

What was the voice that Welty heard? She implied a discernible, constantly reliable authenticity that resides in language and that transcends the personality of the writer, though the writer's personality speaks in every line. The source of this authenticity is the rhythmic nature of language—the voice of literature. When one reads Jane Austen, Virginia Woolf, Tolstoy, or any other great writer, one literally hears and experiences the presence of the author and simultaneously experiences what occurs only when a work has transcended the purely personal and risen to the sphere of the universal. The recognition doesn't require rationalization. You know it when you hear it, instantly, always. And so it was when Ray and I shared "Sonny's Blues"—Wow! What a great story!

For the following discussion, if the reader has not read "Sonny's Blues" or not read it lately, I recommend pausing now to read it before continuing on with this book. "Sonny's Blues" can be found in James Baldwin's story collection *Going to Meet the Man* and in the *American Short Story Masterpieces* anthology.

Reading is good; rereading is better. I can't say with certainty how many times—forty? fifty?—I've read "Sonny's Blues," only that for more than thirty-five years I've been reading and teaching the story to writers who are developing their art. In classes I ask students to read their works aloud, and I read aloud the work of the writers we're studying. Good writing has a rhythm that embodies the characters' lives moment to moment and provides the narrator's mediating presence. In editorial and classroom discussions of work, a comment sometimes comes that a beat has been missed—literally, it's a heartbeat. The heartbeat is the syllable, the breath is the line. Not all heartbeats and breaths are the same, of course. The muscular activity of uttering sound springs from the emotional and intellectual experience of life. Words proceed from a unity of mind, body, idea, and emotion. Before words reach the page, the writer locates the core of each rhythmic phrase and lets it come to life so that it touches and quickens the reader's heart. Without this connection between writer and reader, the other elements of writing fall flat.

When I ask students to read their work aloud and a piece isn't working well, I sometimes stop listening to the words and listen instead to the thrum of the voice. Is it coming from the head only, or is it coming from the center of the body, from the heart and loins and stomach as well as the head? What are the moods, prevailing emotions, needs, or desires being expressed? Do they correlate naturally and spontaneously, with the words riding the rhythms, or are the words and rhythms forced, and if so, why, and how might the utterance be improved? How aware is the writer of what the writing imparts to the reader? Is the writer asking the reader to receive ennui, fear, anxiety, irritation, gloom, or confusion unalloyed by hope, affirmation, joy, sympathy, or love? How might the writer come into contact with the impulses driving the work and make more conscious, or at least more effective, choices about the play of language?

Coleridge's definition of poetry—the best words in the best order[4]—applies to prose as well, and if a story succeeds, the words carry the reader all the way home, back to life outside the story, having received gifts along the way. "Sonny's Blues" is such a story, an eternal one, a masterpiece that requires no explanation, yet there's pleasure in observing how and why Baldwin wrote a story that's long been read in schools everywhere, illuminating human experience and influencing civilization for the better.

[4] Samuel Taylor Coleridge and Henry Nelson Coleridge, *Specimens of the Table Talk of Samuel Tayler Coleridge* (London: John Murray, 1836; Project Gutenberg, 2005), https://www.gutenberg.org/cache/epub/8489/pg8489.html.

ACT I

The primary formal element of "Sonny's Blues" is diction—the lyric movement of language. The title says it—the piece moves on its music, specifically jazz. Baldwin published the story in 1957, at age thirty-three, though he would have been forming the story well before its publication, and it might be said that thirty-three years, or the whole of his lifetime, went into the story. Readers today coming for the first time to this story of Harlem life and heroin addiction, or rereading the story after long years, might view it in contemporary terms, and there's no harm in that. The messages in the story are as old as the biblical allusions Baldwin employs in the contrast between darkness and light, and as evergreen as ordinary human emotions, yet it's well to recall that in 1957 there was no Civil Rights Act, the struggle over Jim Crow laws and segregation had a long way to go, and racial conditions and inequalities were deplorable and disregarded by most white Americans. "Sonny's Blues" issues a prophetic warning about the outcome of racism while making deeply felt gestures of hope and reconciliation. Whenever I read "Sonny's Blues," I think of John Coltrane's "A Love Supreme," a long, prayerful piece that gives thanks for his recovery from heroin addiction and that percussively, sonorously refrains its title in praise of the Creator. Coltrane's song dates from 1963, a few years after "Sonny's Blues," and both pieces take part in a shift occurring in race consciousness and the American psyche. "A Love Supreme" proceeds in four parts—Acceptance, Resolution, Pursuance, and Psalm—a similar orchestration to "Sonny's Blues," which occurs in three acts across thirty-two pages and begins with a song of denial:

> I read about it in the paper, in the subway, on my way to work. I read it, and I couldn't believe it, and I read it again. Then perhaps I just stared at it, at the newsprint spelling out his name, spelling out the story. I stared at it in the swinging lights of the subway car, and in the faces and bodies of the people, and in my own face, trapped in the darkness which roared outside.
>
> It was not to be believed and I kept telling myself that, as I walked from the subway station to the high school.

The narrator does not immediately reveal what "it" is or who it's about, and ordinarily this withholding would constitute a potential error in storytelling, an assumption that readers will pursue the story to find out what's going on, whereas faced with obliquity, readers make what associations they can and begin telling themselves a story that is likely somewhat other than the one intended by the author. But the occasion of "Sonny's Blues" is that a longstanding denial of a horribly painful truth has come home to the main character and can no longer be denied, though he tries. Having established this conflict, Baldwin promptly reveals the news: the narrator's younger brother, Sonny, has been arrested for using and peddling heroin. The mortal impact of the news puts the reader in immediate contact with the heart of the story, and from that moment nothing further is withheld from the reader, and the story proceeds with forthcoming directness. What's at stake is life and death.

Many readers may report that the story is told by Sonny's older brother and not necessarily observe that the narrator is a slightly older, significantly altered person from who he'd been before he read the news of Sonny's arrest. His role as narrator is not identical to his role as a character in the story. Employing the differences between the *I* who lived the story and the *I* who tells it is a time-honored technique equally observable in classic stories such as James Joyce's "Araby" and in contemporary masterpieces such as Tobias Wolff's "The Liar" and Alice Munro's "Lying Under the Apple Tree." The principle involved in the technique is that the diction and perspective of the narrator is not, and should not be, only identical to that of the character(s). This distinction operates in all adroit uses and persons of point of view—first, second, limited third, and omniscient. Baldwin didn't invent the technique; he observed it in works he read, learned it, and in "Sonny Blues" deploys it to great effect. The most natural and easiest way to achieve the effect occurs through the benefit of the passage of time and reflection that has occurred beyond the events of the story—in this case, a retrospective first-person narration. The implicit distinction between the then of the events and the now of the telling provides Baldwin with the means of creating dramatic irony,[1] tension, and an open framework, or structure, that any reader can inhabit with clear, steady comprehension. Readers need not observe how the effect is achieved but only experience its result. The narration is the older brother's confession, his apology, and the reader is its beneficiary.

[1] *Dramatic irony* is the term of art for the device by which the reader knows and understands more than do the characters living in the moments of the story. The reader experiences the moments with the characters and simultaneously has a superior view. This element provides the reader with a steady sense of pleasure.

> I read about it in the paper, in the subway, on my way to work. I read it, and I couldn't believe it, and I read it again.

The tonal precision and momentum alternating with resistance in the first few phrases instantly communicates interest, desire, shock, confusion, suffering, and tenderness. The sounds of struggle enter the reader, and images quickly follow.

> I stared at it in the swinging lights of the subway car, and in the faces and bodies of the people, and in my own face, trapped in the darkness which roared outside.

The musicality of the piece, which will gradually grow into a full-on jazz performance, begins with a few sounds and details, as the older brother feels, hears, and sees more than he wants to see, in particular his own face trapped in darkness, an image that echoes a Bible verse from First Corinthians 13:12:

> For now we see in a mirror dimly, but then face to face. Now I know in part; then I shall know fully, even as I have been fully known.

In avoiding the truth about his addicted brother, the older brother has successfully avoided himself. In stories, characters either connect and more accurately know themselves and others, or they don't, and it's not all or nothing but to what degree and how the connection occurs or fails. The implicit contract with the reader is that either the characters will make connections or, to the extent that they don't, the connections will be made via the presence of the narrator so that the reader will not end in a state of loss and confusion, though the characters may continue to struggle. From the opening of "Sonny's Blues," readers instinctively understand that the brothers must encounter one another and wrestle with the truth, failing which there's no story, no meaningful outcome. The storytelling principle involved is that everything latent in the characters should come forward into outward drama by the end of the story.

The narrator tells us, "I was scared, scared for Sonny." The repetition of *scared* with an emphasis that the fear was *for Sonny* expresses a resistance in the older brother, as if he has no cause to be afraid for himself but only for Sonny. Lyric inflection and tone combined within the narrator's retrospective point of view skillfully embody the tension in the difference between Sonny's reality and the self-protective if nonetheless concerned and now upset version of reality that the older brother has long inhabited. The plot destination of the narrator's point of view is toward recognition, and all along the arc of the story there will be reversals, progress and regress, the lens of consciousness opening and closing and opening again so that in the aggregate the outcome will be either for better or for worse. But the narrator already knows how it turned out, and the quality of his utterance implicitly expresses the nature of the outcome without removing the desire and drama in getting to the ending.

Sonny's brother is a high school algebra teacher, and amid teaching his classes, he feels a block of ice melting, sending trickles of ice water up and down his veins, and expanding until he feels his guts will spill and he'll choke or scream in moments when he remembers Sonny as a boy the age of his students. Sonny's face "had been bright and open, there was a lot of copper in it; and he'd had wonderfully direct brown eyes, and great gentleness and privacy." Among all the words to describe brown or Black, Baldwin chooses *copper*, and whether the choice was made intuitively or deliberately, it's telling. Copper is the most conductive of all metals, and Sonny, the reader will gradually discover, is likewise conductive. This descriptive detail, like all the other details in the story, is essential but doesn't call attention to itself. It plays its literal part within the naturalistic tapestry of life while also accreting in a meaningful pattern of imagery.

Reflecting on the light going out of Sonny's face in his teenage years, the narrator draws a conclusion:

> These boys, now, were living as we'd been living then, they were growing up with a rush and their heads bumped abruptly against the low ceiling of their actual possibilities. They were filled with rage. All they really knew were two darknesses, the darkness of their lives, which was now closing in on them, and the darkness of the movies, which had blinded them to that other darkness, and in which they now, vindictively, dreamed, at once more together than they were at any other time, and more alone.

Note the precision with which the narrator names the circumstance. For all the rage, darkness, and alienation expressed, the tone is dispassionate; the writing, clear and precise. A reader's feelings enter the passage because the language isn't emotive or prejudiced, telling a reader what to feel. What's described is done matter-of-factly, and the effect is breathtaking.

In a reader's mind the images materialize as if acted out directly onstage before the reader's eyes—the low ceiling, the abrupt collision against it, the claustrophobic doubling of the darkness, one within the other, and now not just the older brother's face and Sonny's face mirrored but the societally obscured faces of the quarter million Black people in Harlem in the 1950s and the 12 million in the US. In Baldwin's telling the images are more powerful than the numbers they represent, or rather the images amplify the significance of the numbers by focusing them in terms of individual lives. Anyone among those numbers in the 1950s, and anyone from then to now living under racial oppression, would recognize the truth of Baldwin's images and experience an affirmation of the dreadful reality of their lives. And anyone not of those numbers yet alive at heart can feel the injustice and tragedy, without Baldwin preaching or pleading.

Harlem's demography from the nineteenth century forward sets the background for "Sonny's Blues." The predominately Jewish and Italian population of Harlem began to change in the early twentieth century with the migration of African Americans fleeing the Jim Crow South. In 1910 the Black population of Harlem was 10 percent. By 1930 it was 70 percent. During World War I, industries recruited Black laborers, but during the decade of the Great Depression, unemployment in Harlem grew very high, and more so for men than women.[2] Poverty, crime, and drug use escalated. In the 1950s the New York City rate of death from heroin use for Black users was as much as two times higher than for white users, and the median age of those who died was twenty-seven. The mortality rate from heroin for Black users in Harlem was 50 percent higher than for Black users elsewhere in the US.[3] Throughout these decades in Harlem, many landlords preferred renting to tenants who could afford only cheap rents, which in turn relieved landlords from keeping up their properties. In the 1930s and 1940s, rent strikes and incidents of

[2] Wikipedia, s.v. "Harlem," last modified September 4, 2022, 4:23, https://en.wikipedia.org/wiki/Harlem.

[3] Colin McCord and Harold P. Freeman, "Excess Mortality in Harlem," *New England Journal of Medicine* (January 18, 1990), https://www.nejm.org/doi/full/10.1056/nejm199001183220306; Matt Kautz, "The State Versus Harlem," *Gotham Center for New York History*, April 11, 2019, https://www.gothamcenter.org/blog/the-state-versus-harlem; Blanche Frank, "An Overview of Heroin Trends in New York City," *Mount Sinai Journal of Medicine* (October/November 2000), https://wmich.edu/sites/default/files/attachments/u372/2015/An%20Overview%20of%20Heroin%20Trends_1.pdf.

rioting and violence ensued. And for Harlem residents, having an education was not necessarily a protection from want and despair. Employment for Black workers tended to go more to the unskilled, uneducated laborers than to the educated. These various conditions reinforced one another. Among other New York City boroughs and other cities in the US, Harlem offered its children a very low quality of education. This is the environment that surrounds the older brother as he teaches his high school students algebra.

The school bell rings, the last class ends. A day has passed between the morning's subway ride and the afternoon, all within little more than a page, and within that day entire lifetimes have been evoked and urgently carried forward on the escalating tension of the older brother's anxiety and the narrator's illuminations about the lives in the story. Narrative and commentary are interwoven, which is to say that the skillful performance of a story depends on *show and tell* rather than the often cited writing workshop instruction, *show, don't tell,* designed primarily to encourage beginning writers to dramatize and to inhibit exposition and explaining, which play flat unless alloyed with other elements such as patterns of imagery, plot, theme, characterization, refraction of point of view showing what moves between and within characters, and the lyric play of language embodying characters' emotions, each phrase of a story doing more than it literally says. Baldwin combines elements and, word to word, keeps the beat, playing a full keyboard of life's notes as if effortlessly and with an effect of spontaneity, making each line an expressive measure of time, no less than an accomplished musical composer would. And here, rather than drive the story forward from its evocation of adolescent urgency meeting relentlessly defeating odds that produce dreams of revenge, Baldwin creates a pause in the transition from one scene to the next. All the energy, or power, accumulated to this point in the story gathers before shifting dynamically to a new movement, as is necessary from scene to scene in effective story writing. The older brother lets out his breath. His clothes are wet, as though he's been sitting in a steam bath. At the end of the school day, he sits a long time alone in his classroom and listens to the boys outside, shouting, cursing, laughing. All this occurs in a few quick sentences that nonetheless carry a weight of endurance, and in the space between the older brother's stillness and the commotion outside, unsettling perceptions well up.

> Their laughter struck me for perhaps the first time. It was not the joyous laughter which—God knows why—one associates with children. It was mocking and insular, its intent was to denigrate. It was disenchanted, and in this, also, lay the authority of their curses. Perhaps I was listening to them because I was thinking about my brother and in them I heard my brother. And myself.

The passage strikes a revelatory balance between knowing and unknowing, between what the older brother had been unwilling to know at the time and what he now admits and continues to struggle with in the telling, as well as between what the boys know and their limited means to express, much less alter, any of it.

Their laughter struck me for perhaps the first time is a rising line buoyed by the boys' youthful energy and the listener's sense of discovery. The next line dips down with negation *It was not,* and then it lifts simply on *joyous laughter*—words do what they say—which sets the tone for the aside *God knows why*. It's a complexly ironic phrase that plays humbly and cannot be misheard. *God* with its glottal *G* exhaling the short *o* sounding *ah/awe* into the commanding palatal *d* is a bass note springing to and holding under the bright round opening of *knows*, a tenor horn softly curling a muted cry in on itself *why*, and who can say with certainty how consciously or instinctively Baldwin formed each line as he wrote the story, but definitely he was hearing the lines and feeling how each bit connected to the characters and could touch a reader. Baldwin's ear was as fine as a tuning fork to bring perfect pitch to his tongue. From his early teenage years as a Pentecostal preacher, he possessed precocious oratorical skills that powerfully moved an audience in call and response, and when as a young man he left the pulpit and dedicated himself to writing, he carried his gifts with him. After he became a well-known writer, he sometimes likened himself in interviews to blues or jazz artists rather than to literary ones, though he was well read and practiced in literary forms.

At this point in "Sonny's Blues," the reader isn't thinking about musical effects, isn't aware of hearing jazz or blues in the scraps of sound that will ultimately crescendo in a transcendent performance at a Village nightclub, but that's where the story will finish, and naturally so because directed causal movement, details, notes, and the path have been provided, without requiring the reader to do more than receive the impressions given moment to moment.

God knows why tenderly confides existential doubt. It interrupts the continuity between two phrases—*joy and laughter* and *one associates with children*—and from the break in the assumed cause-and-effect relationship between joy and childhood, Baldwin subtly employs the pronoun *one* to invoke a shared human condition. The pronoun is both personal and impersonal, and having used it here, and having brought the reader into his confidence, Baldwin can later more easily employ the collective first-person *we*, always a tricky word as it can arouse quibbling, if not outright contention, in a reader who may not agree with being included in a particular group of others—for instance, a white reader, on the one hand, and Black American experience, on the other. Chekhov noted that the storyteller's role is not to answer the question but to state it correctly—that is, stories are based on questions that cannot be answered absolutely but only embodied in the meaningful playing out of paradoxes in the lives of the characters. The metaphysical question in "Sonny's Blues" is, *Why do we suffer?* Typically, in good stories the metaphysical question is expressed in one of three ways, and often in all three ways—by direct dramatic action, out of the mouths of the characters, and in commentary from the narrator. Baldwin adroitly calls on all three methods and will open out the *why* in *God knows why* when the brothers are finally able to confront each other and Sonny speaks his truth beyond any denying. In the meantime, Baldwin has let the reader hear the narrator's muted sorrow and resignation, his exhaustion born of endless mortification, his reasonable courage and assertiveness with a flicker of scorn at self and God in the face of fate, the overall effect of the phrase combining disillusion and hope. It's worth noting as well that by placement in the sentence and by tone, Baldwin has taken an otherwise cliché *God knows why* and made it ring with new life. The familiarity of the phrase offers comfort in an assumed commonality of understanding, while the originality of its use in context and its inflections disturb expectation and elicit deeper engagement.

In the rising and falling action of the story, each line is a drama of its own and has a shape of its own, the line thereby adding more strongly to the cumulative effect, or integrity, of the story than if the line were more dependent on the preceding or the following line for its own effect. Transitions are key in how well a reader can follow, or track, a story word by word and line by line, with clear sound and sense. The end of a sentence carries the most emphasis, by virtue of being the end, and the line ending on *children* lifts to carry a reader affirmatively into the tempered fierceness of the narrator's conclusive penetration of what the curses and laughter mean.

> It was mocking and insular, its intent was to denigrate. It was disenchanted, and in this, also, lay the authority of their curses. Perhaps I was listening to them because I was thinking about my brother and in them I heard my brother. And myself.

Having long been overinvested in self-certainties, and confronted by the cutting realities around him, the older brother grows shaky in his isolation and has little alternative but to reflect on himself. Recalling all this, the narrator's care toward his former self and his brother, along with his confessed uncertainty indicated by *perhaps,* provides the sense that the reader participates in thinking through what's happening. The restraint, dignity, openness, and humility of the older brother's utterance mark that experiencing the story involves learning something worth knowing and being altered by the outcome.

Denigrate—literally, to blacken—connotes what society has done to the boys and caused them do to themselves in the calamitous hierarchy of self-worth based on shades of color. Baldwin doesn't blame, though well he might (to the detriment of the story). He lets the descriptors do their resonant work. They need no explanation or emphasis beyond their emergence in the flow of the narrative. Whether or not a reader immediately grasps all that's contained in each word and phrase, the lines create visceral impact.

Disenchantment, or disillusion, grounds the *authority* of the boy's curses, emitted against the societally enforced cruelty of their lives. In speaking about the boys, the narrator speaks for them, lending their curses more meaningful articulation and thus according the boys their truth. The older brother approaches this truth as he thinks about his brother and himself, but then he hears a boy outside whistling a tune.

> At once very complicated and very simple, it seemed to be pouring out of him as though he were a bird, and it sounded very cool and moving through all that harsh, bright air, only just holding its own through all those other sounds.

This distraction creates another pause and a moment of relief after the concentrated challenge of recognition in the preceding movement. The tune seems a spontaneous manifestation of a natural self, whose motif takes shape and threads itself through the chaos. As the story progresses, the motif will grow, and the *bird* will reappear, though so transformed a reader may not recall the earlier instance of the *bird* or need to recognize how the author has achieved the effect of the imagery. It simply works, first and obviously in literal details and then symbolically in a cumulative pattern.

Poised at the threshold of awareness, what the older brother hears in the tune is a possibility of restoration, though in that moment he dissociates from thinking about himself. The pause and dissociation are part of a dramatic structure in which scenes are composed of short movements of conflict, action, and resolution, with reversals—rising and falling action, progress and regress—occurring apace. Characters in stories, as with individuals in life, are not always able to discern what's most important and why. But Baldwin keeps the reader in the heart of the story, and like the reader's heart, the story proceeds by contraction and dilation. A reading from the *I Ching* applies:

> The heart is constantly moving.
> The heart's movements are thoughts.
> It is important to pay attention to the immediate situation.
> To do otherwise only makes the heart sore.[4]

Emotional truths transpiring moment to moment in the characters' lives form the sentences that carry a reader. As Cynthia Ozick notes, "Ideas are emotions that penetrate the future of coherence."[5] Each sentence moves from the known into the unknown, carrying the reader forward as in life, though with a more focused plot than is often apparent in life. Aristotle's definitions of *reversal* and *recognition* describe the action of plot.[6] A *reversal* is a change in fortune from good to bad, or from bad to good. *Good* and *bad* are relative terms. A character may move from a circumstance that is not so bad or really quite bad to one that is better or worse, or may shift from being in a good or so-so situation to one that is better or worse. Reversals occur at many points along the axis between the absolute extremes of good and bad. The terms *good* and *bad* are also relative in the sense that what

[4] *I Ching*, trans. Richard Wilhelm and Cary F. Baynes (Princeton: Princeton University Press, 1977), 202.

[5] Cynthia Ozick, "Pear Tree and Polar Bear: A Word on Life and Art," *Metaphor & Memory* (New York: Vintage, 1980), 111.

[6] Aristotle, *Poetics*, trans. James Hutton (New York: Norton, 1982), 55.

is good or bad for one character may not be so for another. The movement of reversal, then, is toward an improved or worsened state of being, a rising or falling of fortune and fate as concerns each character and the relationships between characters.

Recognition is the discovery of new knowledge or insight, or the recovery of lost knowledge, that results in greater friendship or enmity with others and, consequently, a change in fortune from good to bad, or from bad to good. By this definition, it can be seen that recognition implies reversal, and likewise that reversals come about in part according to a character's degree of understanding or ignorance of the meaning and consequence of circumstances, thoughts, desires, actions.

Aristotle draws a distinction between simple and complex stories. A simple story demonstrates reversal without recognition occurring; a complex story produces both reversal and recognition. Among the many thousands of stories published each year, simple stories preponderate, for the reason that it is easier to dramatize events and actions than to illuminate them meaningfully. "Sonny's Blues" is a wonderfully complex story, made so by Baldwin's depth of human understanding, which inspires his characterizations.

The whistled tune reaches the older brother's ears by happenstance yet has an understated effect of miracle, as if risen from his soul's desire. He stands up, goes to the window, and looks down into the school courtyard. It's spring and the sap's rising in the boys. Teachers pass through the courtyard, uneasy and eager to get away from the troubling boys. The older brother collects his things, getting ready to go home to his wife, Isabel. *Home, Isabel,* and *window,* quietly given as destinations and recurring through the story, orient the reader along the brothers' path.

The older brother goes down into the courtyard and encounters not the whistling boy but a grownup boy Sonny's age, an old friend of Sonny's who looks something like him, but this boy is no one that the older brother wants to see.

The boy is "always high and raggy," hanging around with excuses for needing money, which the older brother always gives him. The older brother tells us, in a sighing tone of resignation, that he doesn't know why he gives him money. And we sense that it's not that he doesn't know, it's that he doesn't want to know. The long habit of denial persists in him. Though well-characterized in the scene to follow, the boy is unnamed, and his namelessness reflects his condition in society. Toni Morrison noted:

> The Black community is a pariah community. Black people are pariahs. The civilization of Black people that lives apart from but in juxtaposition to other civilizations is a pariah relationship. In fact, the concept of the Black in this country is almost always one of the pariah. But a community contains pariahs within it that are very useful for the conscience of that community.[7]

Within a pariah community there are degrees of exclusion or perceived deplorability. To be nameless is to be as if invisible, overlooked, out of mind. Sonny's friend showing up as he does troubles the older brother's conscience. His determined unwillingness to know about the boy draws us toward the end of the first movement of a three-and-a-half-page scene composed of eight short movements of conflict, action, and resolution, each movement a progressive stage in a confrontation that moves the older brother closer to the truth about his brother and himself.

[7] Toni Morrison, interview, in *Black Women Writers at Work*, ed. Claudia Tate (New York: Continuum, 1984), 129.

Baldwin brings the boy onstage at this juncture in the story as a messenger, an intermediary before the two brothers face each other, and this bit of delay and stagecraft allows a greater buildup of drama and revelation than if Baldwin had instead brought the brothers together sooner.

Baldwin transitions into the second movement of the scene with the brother allowing that he hates the boy, likening him to a dog or a cunning child, and wonders what the hell he's doing in the schoolyard. The boy shuffles over, the verb *shuffle* adding a plaintive tone to the dialogue: the boy says he sees that the older brother has the newspaper and already knows about Sonny.

The brother acidly responds, "How come they didn't get you?"

The boy has brought news that the brother and the reader already know, and generally a skilled author will not repeat what a reader already knows unless the repetition transforms and furthers the story. Here the repetition adds impact by giving the news greater external reality via the boy, who embodies aspects of Sonny that elicit emotions and perceptions arriving against the brother's will. He tries to shuck the boy off, as anyone might, not wanting to deal with a beggar junkie, but the boy companionably says he'll walk the brother *a little ways,* a colloquial expression with biblical resonance, joining the two characters in awkward need on life's journey. Like a shadow, the boy sticks with the brother, who grows uncomfortably aware that some of his students see him walking side by side with a junkie. This physical conjunction, which marks the conclusion of the second movement of the three-page scene, quietly yet dynamically transfers the growing power and energy of the story into the next movement.

The boy jarringly asks what the brother's going to do about Sonny. The question is Baldwin's version of the brother's keeper motif from the Cain and Abel story in Genesis, and when the brother, like Cain, angrily acts as if there's nothing he can do, the boy quickly echoes resignation and, as if with innocent irony, the impossibility of help. The brother's inward reaction is to reject the boy's right to say that Sonny can't be helped.

It's too early in the story for the reader to know for sure whether or not anything can be done for Sonny, though the natural human instinct for hope has been aroused in the reader. Meanwhile, the older brother and the raggy boy each struggle to hold a portion of dignity against the white world's overwhelming odds. So the third movement in the scene ends in relative equipoise in the moral positions of the two characters. The boy is a bearer of the truth, but degraded by addiction, he fronts a guilefully self-protective meekness, while the brother holds himself as superior. However, the narration—that is, the older brother's confession—provides sufficient perspective and transparency for readers to appreciate the impostures and ironies at play.

The brother's denial of Sonny pushes the question of responsibility back onto the boy, and the next movement, the fourth in the scene, opens with the boy musing aloud but as if to himself that he thought Sonny was too smart to get caught. The comment ruffles the brother's defenses, his sense of his own smarts, and he answers sharply that Sonny probably thought he was smart too and likely the boy thinks he's smart too, at which the boy rawly admits that if he were smart he'd have shot himself a long time ago—immediate self-destruction rather than slow death on the needle. This nakedly miserable self-loathing offends the brother and frightens him more than he knows, because his method of survival has been to avoid knowing. Also, in the mix of the interaction, the addict's tinge of self-pitying defensiveness, emotional challenge, and manipulation, signifying *I'll show you what's real if you can face it,* spark the brother's indignation and anger. He reviles the boy, as anyone resting on superiority and pride for a sense of safety might, and says if it were up to him he'd give him the gun, in essence wishing the boy dead, a reaction that any unthinking person offended by or frightened of the addict might wish, with an instinctively defensive rationalization that the boy created his own misery and deserves it. But as soon as the older brother has lashed out, he feels guilty at scorning the boy and quickly asks what will happen to Sonny.

This gesture provides for a mutual opening between the two characters, a pivotal moment midpoint in the scene, a symmetry, initiating a fifth movement, in which the boy goes inward, reflecting on the past and confessing responsibility for having told Sonny, when they were in school, that heroin felt great. The older brother listens more carefully as the two men stop at a subway station on a corner. The boy peers into the open doorway of a bar, seeming to look for someone, evoking in the reader the worry that the boy is scouting for his next fix or needs to avoid someone. A jukebox is blasting in the bar, a barmaid is laughing and dancing, and the brother sees in her the little girl she once was and senses the "doomed, still struggling woman beneath the battered face of the semi-whore." Baldwin's swift, graceful description, a tableau vivant, reveals the woman's life span, her fate in Harlem—beginning, middle, and end. Baldwin accords the boy and the barmaid their own lives as distinct from being only functions of the brother's story, and by expressing these characters via the brother's recognitions as his long-held denials incrementally dissolve, Baldwin brings readers into an intimate felt experience of shared humanity. A reader unfamiliar with the world Baldwin shows, or a reader inclined to suppress awareness of it, may nonetheless accord and identify with the brother's observations and thus with him. His condition has been forced on his race by the white world and inculcated through generations, and a previously unaware or antipathetic reader may be moved in the course of the story to accept the unwelcome truth of injustice and his or her part in it. In the sixty-five years since Baldwin first published the story, millions of readers have been so moved.

When teaching "Sonny's Blues," I sometimes manage to get all the way through the lecture without letting my voice break or my tears well, though never without some students' tears. But what are these tears? Grief, of course, at the terrible suffering. Wonder at the endurance required for survival and self-respect. Sorrow and joy mingled when the vulnerable heart's truth is called forth, touched and held without sentimentality. Gratitude for Baldwin's art.

As the brother stands on the Harlem corner, seeing the barmaid and hearing the jukebox, he feels as if the pavement shakes under his feet—that is, his legs are shaking. His world shakes, and hearing the boy's confession, the brother feels carried somewhere he doesn't want to go, and the narrator says, "I certainly didn't want to know how it felt. It filled everything, the people, the houses, the music, the dark, quicksilver barmaid, with menace, and this menace was their reality." The punctuated cadence of these lines carries the weight of overwhelming menace, and within the cadence inflected turns of syllable and phrase flicker with troubled life, while the tone remains calm. The brother doesn't want to go there, and when the narrator ascribes the menace as "their reality," he signals the brother's resistance to what he's living in, as if he's not part of it all, yet he's already there and so are we.

Here, at the resolved moment of the fifth movement in the ongoing scene, it's worth pausing to ask if anything that's been told and shown so far in the story is obscure, vague, incomprehensible? Is anything absent, causing incomprehension or misunderstanding? No. Everything has been provided, and will continue to be provided, so that any idiot can understand the story. And I count myself among the idiots. The story must carry the reader; the reader will not, cannot, carry the story for the author. If a story's surface, or primary level, has clarity and integrity, readers can receive the story's depths and complexities; but if the idiot level isn't working, then readers are unlikely to see beyond it or to keep reading. All that Baldwin gives, he gives generously—but neither too much nor too little. Implicitly, readers trust him and his reasonable authority in the telling. Baldwin's rhetoric, his use of formal elements—diction, point of view, characterization, patterns of imagery, plot, and theme—communicates clearly and consistently so that, without having to think or decipher, readers know how to read the story.

The sixth movement of the scene begins almost as if in a whisper escaping from beneath the weight of menace and resistance. The brother asks again what will happen to Sonny, which is something a reader wants to know too.

The boy casually explains that after Sonny's been locked up, treated, and released, he'll just work his way back into addiction. The brother understands but acts as though he doesn't, and the boy chides him sarcastically while holding a calm, patient attitude of one long familiar with willfully blind eyes. The brother, sensing that the boy barely holds himself together, feels again the ice in his belly—the *dread* he's been holding. Flannery O'Connor defined writing as the accurate naming of the things of God.[8] In her definition, *things* includes all things essential to a story and its characters, especially the emotional truths that transpire. Baldwin, by precisely naming what the brother has been experiencing and avoiding, connects, affirms, and sharpens a reader's emotional understanding to this point in the story and casts the meaning of the experience forward. The brother asks if the boy means Sonny will never kick the habit, and the boy concurs:

> That's right, he said cheerfully. *You* see what I mean.

The contrapuntal use of the adverb *cheerfully* is a brilliant, simple touch that adds unexpected tone and characterization. A lesser writer might have omitted an adverb or used one that would emphasize the heaviness of the moment rather than lifting and illuminating it. The principle involved in the writing is that when things are heavy in a story, it's best to write light. Thus the movement that began on a down note of menace ends on a paradoxical up note of recognition that carries into the short seventh movement of the scene, wherein the brother desperately asks why Sonny wants to die.

The question surprises the boy, who responds, "Don't nobody want to die, ever." Notice that Baldwin gives each character a unique voice, and he carefully, sparingly employs idiomatic gestures so that idiom doesn't overshadow the characters and so that a reader's ear, catching the gestures, understands and fills in more of the sound. Now the brother wants to ask more

[8] Flannery O'Connor, *The Habit of Being*, ed. Sally Fitzgerald (New York: Farrar, Straus & Giroux, 1979), 126, 128.

questions but fears the answers and instead starts walking, saying in his superior way that all of it is none of his business, which constitutes a reversal or regressive movement after degrees of openness between the two men.

Consequently, the eighth and final movement of the scene begins with the boy resuming his customary persona of helplessness. He pretends that he accidently left his money at home and asks to borrow a dollar from the brother for a couple of days. Earlier, in the first movement of the scene, the narrator recalled the boy's characteristic begging and the brother's usually giving in to it in spite of his resentment, and so when it happens here it plays as a natural and inevitable conflict. But this time, after the fraught conversation about Sonny has touched the brother's vulnerabilities, the boy's request pierces the brother's core, and he feels as if everything in him, all his tears, will pour out, and he doesn't hate the boy. The brother doesn't have a dollar, only a five, which he hands over. The boy's face closes in shame, and he quickly parts, with the pretense that he'll write to Sonny and that he'll be seeing the brother. While it's very unlikely that the boy will write to Sonny—the boy says it as a kind of apology—it's indeed likely that he and the brother will run into each other again, but the boy will not reappear in the story. In effect, his fate is sealed, like the fates of so many others who have shared, and who continue to share, his condition. In contrast, Sonny and his brother's fates are more at play, alive with possibility of recognition and recovery. Will they manage to connect? The buoyant heart that Baldwin gives the older brother's narration carries the reader with the desire for and belief in the possibility of life and a better outcome than the surrounding indications of doom.

The three and half pages covering the older brother's encounter with the raggy boy represent a masterly use of dramatic structure, in which the reader is carried on short conclusive movements of conflict, action, and resolution, each movement leading causally to the next one, each movement being a half-page or so in length. The entirety of "Sonny's Blues" is built in this way. Most readers are unlikely to observe this structure but simply experience the alacrity and impact of each movement and the cumulative effect of all the movements together. It's much easier and more effective to carry a reader in this sort of narrative structure than across longer, dramatically uninflected passages of writing.

Ideally, a story moves directly from essential scene to essential scene, without intervening material, which is exactly how "Sonny's Blues" proceeds up to the point when the raggy boy and older brother part ways, but achieving continuously directed dramatic movement along a story line sometimes requires a plot summary bridge between scenes. After the day on which the brother learns about Sonny's arrest and encounters the raggy boy in the schoolyard, Baldwin creates a short bridge to the next direct scene, in which the two brothers will meet for the first time in the story. The bridge consists of the older brother's admission that for a long time he didn't make any effort to contact Sonny in prison, but finally the death of the brother's young daughter prompted him to write to Sonny, who sends a brief letter of condolence and confesses his need for his brother, his regrets, fears, and confusion. He asks the brother to meet him when gets out of prison, and in closing wishes he could have their mother's faith in the Lord's will but, given the world's endless troubles, he can't summon that belief. Sonny's letter makes the brother feel like a bastard for having held himself back from Sonny. The bridge operates as summary but has the added strength of characterization and a religious motif concerning faith and disbelief that will play out in the story. The bridge doesn't present drama occurring with the characters interacting directly onstage, and if the bridge were only summary, it would tend to play flat; instead, Baldwin alloys the summary with character development, theme, and Sonny's voice in the letter, creating tension and impetus across two-thirds of a page that carries the reader into the brothers' reunion.

After writing the first letter, the older brother stays in touch with Sonny, and on Sonny's release from prison, the older brother's first sight of him brings a flood of memories and thoughts about Sonny's inner life. Sonny looks older, thinner, possessed of a deeper, distant, inward stillness and seems unlike what the older brother recalled of his baby brother. When Sonny smiles, the older brother sees him as if for the first time, looking out from his private depths, hoping to be encouraged into the light.

The gestures and dialogue that immediately ensue would in a lesser artist's hands be throwaway—composed of the *handshaking, hello, how are you, I'm fine, good to see you* cliché variety, not doing much, if any, necessary work—but the brothers' past estrangement, the tenuous nature of their reunion, and their need for each other gives strong import to each particle of their interaction, and the reader experiences relief that the first moments go well, and then the reader follows closely to see what will happen.

The older brother relates: "The seven years' difference in our ages lay between us like a chasm: I wondered if these years would ever operate between us as a bridge." It's a gorgeous line, whose eloquence lies in its simplicity of statement and the enantiodromia it enacts, changing the chasm to a bridge. Throughout "Sonny's

Blues" Baldwin poses opposites—dark and light, suffering and joy, denial and acceptance, fear and love—showing the relationship of the extremes and the quicksilver movement between them in human moments. The older brother desires the bridge, so does Sonny, and so does the reader. Character is desire—that is, characters in stories, just like people in real life, are defined and motivated by their needs and desires, and Baldwin knowingly joins the reader's natural desire for completion and community to the characters' desires. But turning the bridge from wish to fulfillment involves overcoming obstacles, so the drama mounts.

The older brother finds that he can hardly breathe, recalling that he was present at Sonny's birth, heard the first words Sonny ever spoke, and caught Sonny just before he fell as he took his first steps, walking from his mother straight to his brother. Here, before the father appears in the story, Baldwin indicates that from birth Sonny's father figure was his brother and that in some ways the father was missing. All this—the breathlessness in an overwhelming rush of memory, the contents of the memories, and the weight of the older brother's familial role finally dawning on him—comes in a single sentence that imparts backstory without stopping the front story.

The success of any story depends on the strength, continuity, and magnitude of its front story. An author's ability to do anything in a story other than front story depends on the success of the front story. The term *front story* describes everything that moves forward in time, following from the moment when the clock starts running at the beginning of a story. *Backstory* indicates anything that comes into a story from a time preceding the immediate forward movement of the front story. The principle involved is that a reader's most profound sense is of his or her own mortality—literally breaths and heartbeats—and a story must create a sense of mortality, of time moving forward to consequence, as great as or greater than the reader's own sense of mortality in order to get the reader to suspend his or her life in favor of the lives in the story. From the first page of "Sonny's Blues," Baldwin has carefully tucked small, essential bits of backstory into the front story so unobtrusively that a reader might scarcely notice that it's happening or how Baldwin does it, and his ability to carry time on the lyric movement of language allows him to extend his use of backstory and reflection when needed as later stages of the story gather critical mass and complexity.

Baldwin displays a dramatist's mastery in accurately portraying his characters' spontaneous interactions and attendant emotions in moments of front running time. Whenever he shifts to backstory he does so with the understanding that the backstory must address a question or desire already aroused in the reader so that the reader wants to go into the backstory and experiences it as essential. Before shifting to backstory, Baldwin makes sure that the drama in the front story is strong enough to carry the reader across the time of the backstory without loss of tension or diminished engagement. In order to maintain a strong pull on the reader, Baldwin employs a keen sense of how long he can stay in backstory and when to return to the front story, never allowing it to attenuate. And he dramatizes each bit of backstory as he would front story so that the backstory plays strongly as a front story of its own. As each portion of backstory plays out, it carries the front story with it, amplifying and advancing it. The reader returns to the front story from the backstory with the understanding that the story and its import have advanced rather than moved backward. All of the story is active; none of it is passive.

Now, as the two brothers head uptown in a cab, their wary reacquaintance loosens up. Recalling Sonny's young teenage wish to be in a better place, the brother lightly asks if Sonny still wants to go to India. Sonny laughs and banters that New York is Indian enough for him. The brother says that the place used to belong to the Indians, and Sonny says they sure knew what they were doing when they sold it. The humor lightens the moment while touching on an image of a fourteen-year-old boy trying to imagine himself into a better world and his brother's rejecting the possibility, each brother trapped. There's a mordant edge to the humor and relief in the frankness between them. The banter also provides a distraction from all they don't yet know how to say to each other; and the lighter notes in the narrator's voice offer an indication that he's no longer completely in denial and, implicitly, subtly that Sonny's outcome in the story will not be tragic. The narrator has already lived through the events in the story. His perspective comes from beyond the end. His touches of humor signal that in the course of events some measure of healing will occur, and without giving away the ending or removing the tension, the older brother narrating (or, rather Baldwin through him) sustains the reader's desire and belief in the possibility of change for the better. The brother silently recalls Sonny reading books about pilgrims meditating naked outdoors in bad weather, walking barefoot on hot coals, seeking wisdom. The brother thought those people were fleeing wisdom, and Sonny, the brother recalls, seemed to look down on him for dismissing the aspiration. This memory humbles the brother, sobering the tone of his narration and returning it to the immediacy of the cab ride and initiating the next movement in the scene.

Sonny hasn't seen the city in a long time, and he asks if they can drive up Central Park West, along the park, and the brother agrees but fears he sounds like he's humoring Sonny and hopes Sonny won't take it that way. With perfect simplicity Baldwin conveys the fluctuations of Sonny's polite sensitivity and his brother's unease. Of the two brothers, Sonny is more natural, spontaneous, and in tune with himself as they try to find a way forward together.

They ride uptown through "the vivid, killing streets" of their childhood. The half-page description of that journey draws directly on Baldwin's own early life. His short book-length essay, *The Fire Next Time*, which first appeared five years after the publication of "Sonny's Blues" and nearly two years ahead of the passage of the Civil Rights Act of 1964—offers insight into why and how Baldwin wrote "Sonny's Blues." Virginia Woolf likened the relationship between life and fiction to

> a spider's web, attached ever so lightly perhaps, but still attached to life at all four corners. Often the attachment is scarcely perceptible; Shakespeare's plays, for instance, seem to hang there complete by themselves. But when the web is pulled askew, hooked up at the edge, torn in the middle, one remembers that these webs are not spun in midair by incorporeal creatures, but are the work of suffering human beings, and are attached to the grossly material things, like health and money and the houses we live in.[9]

Coleridge noted that art is not a copy of life but an imitation—a distinction that invokes the animating power of imagination.[10] "Sonny's Blues" is not autobiography, not literally Baldwin's life,

[9] Virginia Woolf, *A Room of One's Own* (New York: Harcourt, 1929), 43.

[10] Samuel Taylor Coleridge, *Biographia Literaria*, chaps. 17 and 18 (London, 1817; Project Gutenberg, 2004), https://www.gutenberg.org/files/6081/6081-h/6081-h.htm.

not a historical transcription of people and events; instead, the story draws on realities familiar to Baldwin in order to bring into higher relief, illumination, and completion crucial patterns and meanings often obscured, overlooked, or misperceived in the disturbing confusions, apparent randomness, and partial interpretations of daily life. In *The Fire Next Time*, which makes a much more urgently pointed appeal to the American public than was made in "Sonny's Blues," Baldwin recalls the friends of his youth becoming creatures of the street, drinking, smoking, embarking on sexual careers, cursing, fighting, weeping, lost, oppressed, frozen on the needle. As Sonny and his brother ride uptown, Baldwin evokes these same disastrous conditions encircling a current generation of boys. Some escaped, the older brother narrates, but most didn't. And those who did escape left part of themselves behind, "as some animals amputate a leg and leave it in the trap."

The brother has perhaps escaped into his career as a school teacher, and Sonny hasn't lived in Harlem in a long time, yet as the cab carries them "through streets which seemed, with a rush, to darken with dark people"—and here I must pause to note the astonishing power and beauty of the lyric phrasing in that line, the alliteration of instant *d* sounds, the rhythm and imagery tenderly conveying an affinity among people with a sense of love and dread combined—the brother watches Sonny and feels that they are seeking the part of themselves that they'd left behind. The image of Black people on the street leaps wholly formed into the mind's eye, into the reader's heart. Baldwin writes:

> It's always at the hour of trouble and confrontation that the missing member aches.

Baldwin has at will the ability to provide the aphoristic line. It has scriptural resonance but is Baldwin's own. Widely quoted, it can stand apart from the passage in which it occurs, and in context its strength as a culminating line makes the passage leading up to it all the more moving. Baldwin's sincerity of expression, his concision of thought and emotion, and the individuality, clarity, and necessity conveyed via the brother's narration denote Baldwin's truth-telling genius.

As the brothers approach their destination, the narration shifts briefly to present tense. The brother and his family *live* in a relatively new housing project that's already in poor condition—dead grass, thin hedges, big windows that belie small living spaces, TVs in place of an horizon, jaded teens lurking in the playground after dark. Noting the tenants' disregard as contributing to the neglect, the narration resists posing them purely as victims. Baldwin allows for the view of the reader for whom individual will and responsibility define moral worth and state of being. He doesn't judge; he observes. He holds his characters with indifferent sympathy, leaving his readers to judge while being drawn toward fair-mindedness.

In the early 1980s, when Toni Morrison was winding up sixteen years at Random House as a groundbreaking editor of Black authors, I was dismayed to hear various publishing personnel repeat the conventional wisdom of that era: *Black people don't buy books.* It also meant that publishers were reluctant to spend money to support and publish work by Black writers, making it hard for those writers to find an audience. And going back to 1957 and Baldwin's advent, how much more prevalent the conventional notion would have been and how very aware of it Baldwin would have been, taking into account the need to form his work in such a way as to summon an audience by touching readers of all kinds.

The intimacy of the narration has been so well established from the beginning of the story that, throughout the half-page paragraph about where the older brother lives, the present-tense verbs call little attention to themselves but imply a persistent condition. Again note that the time of the telling of the events is from beyond the end of the story but not far past it. *Look,* Baldwin was saying in 1957 in "Sonny's Blues," *this is how things are,* and he wrote with the knowledge that change would be hard and slow to achieve. From then to now, almost seventy years, not all things have improved and some have worsened, and as Baldwin intended, "Sonny's Blues" continues to encourage betterment. Finally, in addition to expanding perspective, the paragraph describing place and circumstance also works as dramatic movement (plot) completing the brothers' literal journey (the cab ride) and their metaphorical one between dire escape and hopeful, frightening return. As the brothers enter the house, the older brother feels he's brought Sonny "into the danger he almost died trying to escape." The *d* alliteration and rhythm of the line echo the earlier aphoristic line and knell together in the story with other *d* sounds—darkness, disenchanted, dread, denigrate, down, die. Ironically, the older brother's self-protecting/self-thwarting habit of denial, even as it gradually weakens, opposes the fatal tolling and bends toward recovery, providing narrative tension that sustains the story and its reader above the threatened fall into an abyss of suffering.

The next scene begins after the arrival at the older brother's apartment. His wife Isabel and their two sons are welcoming and glad to see Sonny, who relaxes. The narrator characterizes

Isabel as being much nicer, more open and giving, than he is. She's gone to a lot of trouble preparing dinner and is able to tease Sonny in a way his brother isn't. Her spirits lift for the first time since the death of their little daughter. But the older brother is filled with dread again, trying to remember all he's ever known about addiction. He's watching Sonny and dying to hear him say he's *safe*.

And that's the end of Act I, all of which is front story, with the exception of about ten lines of backstory references—what Sonny was like as a boy, his fantasy of going to India, the raggy boy's memory of telling Sonny what heroin feels like, and the narrator's brief recall of the brothers' boyhood in Harlem. Each of these bits comes a few short lines at a time and without interrupting the forward pulse of mortal dread and the desire for life that carries the reader.

ACT II

Safe—the final word of Act I repeated as the first word of Act II—provides a buttonhook transition into the second act, which is all backstory and begins with *safe* grunted derisively by the boys' father, who believes there's no place safe for anybody. He was responding to his wife's suggestion that they move to a safer neighborhood. He was often drunk and acting tougher than he actually was, while always wanting something better for the family. But before he found it, he died on a drunken weekend during World War II when Sonny was fifteen. He and the father never got along, because, the brother says, they were a lot alike, with a similar privacy or inner sensitivity.

All this is compactly narrated in a third of a page and sets up a series of nested stories, beginning with the narrator recalling that when he was home on leave just after the father died, his mother tried to tell him something about Sonny. The reader naturally leans in to learn what the mother has to say, but Baldwin suspends that story without losing its tension, as the narrator recalls that the occasion was the last time he saw his mother alive. A useful concept in story writing is: When in doubt, increase the difficulty. And that's what Baldwin's doing here. Amplifying the drama. The front story drive from Act I continues strongly, and the reader's desire deepens with backstory revelations about Sonny and the family.

Baldwin holds the reader in suspense in both the front and back stories, while waiting to hear what the mother will say. But first, the memory of what she had to say brings up another memory, one of when the mother was younger and Sonny and the brother were boys. The narrator summons an image of a living room filled with church folks and relatives after a big Sunday dinner. Everyone is sitting around as night comes on. Occasional street noises and a jangling tambourine from a nearby church fade to quiet. And now the reader is on the hook of three stories at once—the continuing front story tension from the first act concerning the brothers and Sonny's ultimate fate, and whatever the mother wants to impart about Sonny, and most immediately what's going to happen in that living room.

There the adults' faces are darkening like the evening. The mother rocks. The father closes his eyes. Forgotten, the kids lie sleepily on the rug, and in a lap, and curled in a chair in a corner. A hand strokes a child's forehead. The grownups sit around, talking about where they come from, their kinfolk, and all that's happened. The inspiration for this scene can be found in Baldwin's own life, as related in *The Fire Next Time,* and he knows that almost anyone has had similar childhood experiences. The scene extends the light and dark imagery that began on the subway when the older brother read the bad news. The living room scene also extends the characterizations of lost innocence that began with the brother likening his students to himself and Sonny, and the scene adds to the sonic elements that Baldwin gradually orchestrates into the blues of the title. In the course of the story, street noises, churchy sounds, and a jangling tambourine will continue. But soon, in the living room, someone will get up and turn on the light, and the talk will stop. Baldwin writes:

> And when light fills the room, the child is filled with darkness. He knows that every time this happens he's moved just a little closer to that darkness outside. The darkness outside is what the old folks have been talking about. It's what they've come from. It's what they endure. The child knows that they won't talk anymore because if he knows too much about what's happened to them, he'll know too much too soon, about what's going to happen to *him*.

The reader has already witnessed what's going to happen to the children. And here, after evoking a shared human feeling of childhood, Baldwin turns to the specific tragedy that attends Black children in America. It's as if the act of creation—let there be light—reverses itself and brings obliteration. Parents want to protect their children, but for these children there's scant protection other than their parents holding back the ugly truth as long as possible—that is to say, the older brother's habit of denial was inculcated in childhood. He had little, if any, choice about it.

The next scene returns to the first of the nested scenes—the mother wanting to tell her older son something about Sonny. The reader hasn't lost track of it and wants to hear it. There the mother sits in widow's black, humming a church song, "Lord, You Brought Me from a Long Ways Off"—a song that expresses gratitude to God, in spite of life's tribulations. The mother ponders aloud her own death and feels anxious over the fate of her sons. She keeps looking out the window onto the street. The reader knows young Sonny is out there somewhere, though the narration doesn't make it explicit. The tell is in the mother's worrying looks at the window. Where is he? When will he be home? Will he be all right, especially after she's gone? The older brother tries to reassure her that she'll live for a long time and that nothing will happen to Sonny—he's a good boy with good sense.

The mother replies that it's not a question of being good or bad, smart or dumb. Then she reveals the family secret—the third of the nested backstories—the father once had a brother. She looks out the window again and tells the older brother that he never saw his father cry but she did, many times. The older brother is shocked. It's the first time he's seen his mother look old, and he wants to know what happened to the father's brother and why no one ever talked about him.

The mother tells the story in a page of direct dialogue, and Baldwin makes her a really good storyteller. Her diction (voice) is literate and distinct from the sound of the older brother's voice, which is more educated than hers and also at moments a bit pedantic in the manner of a high school teacher. The mother's diction is lightly touched with colloquial phrases—*they was, he don't know, they seen, them white men, weren't nobody, weren't nothing.* She tells the story of the father and his brother on a Saturday night, young men out dancing, singing, drinking; and then walking home under a bright moon, whistling, the brother steps off the road to take a leak. As he steps back on, a car full of drunk white men comes speeding right at him. He freezes and the car rolls over him. The guitar he carries bursts and the strings go flying. The sound of that broken guitar cuts right through the reader, and the mother concludes, "Your Daddy never did really get right again. Till the day he died he weren't sure but that every white man he saw was the man that killed his brother."

Her telling is remarkably absent of blame or judgment. She dries her eyes and tells her son that she doesn't want him to be fearful or to hate anyone but wants him to know that the world hasn't changed.

The older brother doesn't want to believe this. The mother turns away from him, back toward the window. As she watches the street for Sonny, she confides that knowing she held her husband's sorrow keeps her from feeling too downcast. The older brother exclaims that he hadn't known his parents' lives were like that—the emotion of the hidden truth powerfully coming home to him. His mother firmly responds that there's a lot he doesn't know yet but that he's going to find out. And now she tells him what she wanted him to know about Sonny, which the reader has suspensefully waited to hear.

Baldwin casts "Sonny's Blues" as a matriarchal family story, though the brothers are the primary characters. Isabel, Isabel's mother, and the brothers' mother exhibit an authority, knowing, care, and accepted responsibility for being the conduit for relationship in daily moments and across generations. Within a general societal motif in which women are typically seen as more relational than men, Baldwin's matriarchal theme partakes of a narrative in which Black mothers in various ways do their best to protect their sons and husbands from the violence aimed at Black men. The brothers' father experienced firsthand his brother's death brought about by white men. The father never fully recovered and depended on his wife, and on alcohol, to help him through life. Sonny, like the raggy boy, is imperiled by heroin addiction as a means of dealing with suffering. The older brother uses denial to avoid what he doesn't want to know or feel, and there's an implication in his avoidance that, though he's likely a more present father to his children (two sons in addition to the daughter) than his father was for him, Isabel is the heart and nurturing soul of the family. These motifs drawn from life appear in other stories. In particular, I have in mind Edward P. Jones's 2003 short story "All Aunt Hagar's Children." Written five decades after "Sonny's Blues," the Jones story is in a number of ways a descendant of the Baldwin story, especially in terms of making a generative commentary on racial conditions and the future. As the brothers' mother senses her death approaching, her concern is with her sons' future, as Baldwin and Jones are concerned with humankind's future. I'll return to these motifs and to the Jones story toward the end of this book.

The mother's final words to the older brother—what she's been wanting to say to him about Sonny—are a warning and a behest. She says that no matter what happens or how *evil* the older brother gets toward Sonny, she wants the older brother always to be there for Sonny. The mother's use of the word *evil* can be taken as a received colloquial or churchy indicator of all things not *good*. However, the mother's use of the word is precisely knowing. The incremental and wholesale action of evil is to subsume all things unto itself and to negate them. Evil's essence is absence—the ultimate, terrifying darkness and isolation of an abyss. Hence, the mother's injunction that the older brother be present for his brother. And the reader already knows that's the very thing the older brother has failed to do.

The nested scenes comprise three and a half pages, each scene a compact forward movement of conflict, action, and resolution, with a cumulative effect of revelation and the promise of more story, with escalating drama. Having completed those movements, Baldwin makes a plot summary bridge to the next scene. The older brother narrates that two days after the conversation with his mother he was gone until he came back home on special furlough for her funeral. Within the bridge Baldwin includes the older brother's statement that he's had a lot of things on his mind, making him forget his promise to be there for Sonny. The older brother's rationalization to keep himself from feeling guilty supplies an arc of character tension to the plot summary, which would otherwise play flat.

Following a line space, indicating a jump in time, the next scene takes places after the mother's funeral, and the brothers are alone in the mother's empty kitchen. Sonny's still in high school, and the older brother, burdened by an immediate sense of responsibility, asks what Sonny wants to do with his life. What follows is a conversation that could take place between any parental figure and young person, a scene that calls on universal human sympathy while depicting the particular plight of Baldwin's characters.

Sonny says he's going to be a musician. He has a set of drums, so the brother asks if Sonny's going to be a drummer, something the brother thinks is beneath Sonny.

Sonny replies that he doesn't think he'll ever be a really good drummer, but he thinks he can play the piano.

The brother frowns. He's never played the older brother role so seriously, scarcely asked about Sonny at all, and senses his lack of understanding and ability to deal with the situation, all of which makes him frown all the more. He asks what kind of musician Sonny wants to be.

This amuses Sonny. How many kinds of music does the older brother think there are? Sonny laughs at his brother's efforts to classify a type of music, and the brother crossly tells Sonny to be serious, to which Sonny sobers with difficulty, apologizes, and says the brother just sounds so scared, and then Sonny laughs again, making his brother furious.

The older brother narrates that Sonny sobers again, perhaps worried that he's hurt his brother, a telling distinction, given that the older brother has not been at all careful of hurting Sonny's feelings. With halting difficulty, Sonny earnestly admits that he wants to play jazz.

This idea is incomprehensible to the older brother. He can't imagine why Sonny would want to spend his time clowning around on bandstands, putting himself in a class that their father denigrated as "good-time people." While Baldwin doesn't make a point of it, the phrase recalls what the father and his brother were doing on the night the brother died, and it evokes the father's judgment on himself, concealed and passed down to the older brother, while Sonny has instinctively followed an inherited gift and inclination for music. In telling the story of the father's brother's death, the mother said that the white man's car just kept going and "it ain't stopped to this day." It might also be said that the road that the two brothers were on that night is being followed out as a destiny between Sonny and his older brother without their knowing it, yet the nature of that destiny is in their hands and, ultimately, every reader's. Baldwin gradually, gracefully conveys the importance, as well as the difficulty, of individual action and accountability for the fate of all humankind.

The older brother carelessly challenges the idea of Sonny playing jazz, and Sonny looks helpless, annoyed, and deeply hurt, which makes his brother try to be helpful by suggesting that Sonny wants to be like Louis Armstrong.

Sonny's face closes as though he's been struck. He's not interested in any of "that old-time, down home crap," he says.

The brother testily asks who then Sonny admires.

The answer is Bird—Charlie Parker—which picks up and continues the thread started early in the story when the older brother's thoughts were interrupted by a boy whistling a tune

> at once very complicated and very simple, it seemed to be pouring out of him as though he were a bird, and it sounded very cool and moving through all that harsh, bright air, only just holding its own through all those other sounds.

Sonny's avowal of Bird is the midpoint of the story, halfway through the second of three acts. Good storytelling depends on symmetry and balance. Effective story structure holds, carries, orients, and informs the reader without the reader needing to think how it's all being done. Here "Sonny's Blues" subtly shifts and gathers itself toward its culmination, just as the generational evolution from Armstrong's music to Parker's signaled a necessary, often painful struggle to freedom beyond old conventions, styles, modes, expressions, and understandings. An episode in the fourth season of Donald Glover's television show *Atlanta* dramatizes the sometimes fraught progression of racial attitudes in relation to music.[1] In the episode a successful rapper, Paper Boi, finds himself in an Amsterdam nightspot called Cancel Club, where he's somewhat mockingly introduced not by his own stage name but instead as New Jazz, which lands as a multi-edged satire and subtext in a visionary show that's all about race complexity. At the superficial or primary level the appellation New Jazz winkingly says, *Oh, you rap—that's the new jazz.* But the phrase

[1] *Atlanta,* season 3, episode 8, "New Jazz," directed by Hiro Murai, written by Donald Glover, aired May 5, 2022, on FX.

goes back at least to the 1940s and the arrival of bebop, whose intricate melodies originated with Charlie Parker's discovery that the semitones of the chromatic scale can lead to any key, opening greater possibilities for improvisation and carrying jazz beyond the Dixieland and swing-based dance tradition popularized by Louis Armstrong. Sonny's distaste for Armstrong can be read as a younger artist's natural need for self-assertion and transcendence of found forms, much as the young main character of Isaac Babel's short story "Guy de Maupassant" rants against Tolstoy:[2] "He got frightened, our count did! He lacked courage! It was fear that made him turn to religion! Frightened of the cold, of old age, the count knitted himself a jersey out of faith!" There's food for thought in the complaint, but the reader is not meant to take it as earnestly as the impassioned youth who utters it, though his problem is sympathetically recognizable. Teenage Sonny is in effect being asked by his brother to define himself. He feels that his very being is at stake. Baldwin's musical motif embodies the conflict. Wynton Marsalis used two words to define the improvisational nature of bebop and its extension into modal jazz: "I am"—the solo, the individual. By comparison, Marsalis defined the older, foundational form, swing, as: "Other people have personalities, too."[3] Baldwin doesn't necessarily favor one form over another. He offers an evolutionary fusion with the understanding that jazz depends on balance and intimacy because it is a music of conversation and dialogue. In part, "Sonny's Blues" represents a working out of the progress of jazz at three levels—the individual, the

[2] Isaac Babel, "Guy de Maupassant," (1932; *Narrative* 2009), https://www.narrativemagazine.com/issues/spring-2009/masterpieces/guy-de-maupassant-isaac-babel.

[3] André Kimo Stone Guess, *A Conversation with Wynton Marsalis*, Jazz Congress 2018, New York, January 11, 2018, https://wyntonmarsalis.org/news/entry/forgetting-the-roots-of-jazz-is-forgetting-the-history-of-race-in-america.

social, and the mythic. Marsalis has been credited with seeing jazz as a solution to a shared cultural mythology between Blacks and whites that can help move the needle on race relations. Baldwin employs this kind of perception in writing "Sonny's Blues" and was well aware that jazz was the first form of entertainment to be integrated. Beginning in the 1920s with the Jazz Age and the Lost Generation, white musicians took up the new form, which was then said to have been deracinated—a potentially disorienting and ambivalent concept, depending on what lens of perception or interpretation is being applied. Whose music is it? And thinking back a bit further in time, to minstrel shows and blackface, an observer today might recognize in Donald Glover's *Atlanta* episode an intention to highlight Paper Boi's problems of self-identification, integrity, disorientation, and reasonable paranoia within a highly polarized, commodified, all too regressive, cancel-culture atmosphere. Taking a seat at the bar, Paper Boi encounters Liam Neeson, who matter-of-factly expresses hatred of Black people. Neeson's role in the episode alludes to some real-life events in his past, when he was a young man and sought to kill a Black man out of revenge for the rape of one of Neeson's friends. Nothing came of his intention, and he later expressed shame over the inclination, but in playing himself on *Atlanta*, he gave Glover a means of focusing on racial antagonisms. Paper Boi doesn't want to believe what Neeson fronts and says that Neeson must have learned better than to say things like that. Neeson responds that the best and worst part of being white means you don't have to learn anything if you don't want to. Marsalis has called jazz the minstrel show of our time, a comment that alludes both to the diminished place of jazz in popular culture and to the rise of racist attitudes and actions in spite of, and also because of, all progress made. Fear prompts anger and hatred. In *The Fire Next Time* Baldwin noted:

> It is rare indeed that people give. Most people guard and keep; they suppose that it is they themselves and what they identify with themselves that they are guarding and keeping, whereas what they are actually guarding and keeping is their system of reality and what they assume themselves to be. One can give nothing whatever without giving oneself—that is to say, risking oneself. If one cannot risk oneself, then one is simply incapable of giving. And, after all, one can give freedom only by setting someone free.[4]

As a high school and college student, taking part in the social activism and turbulence of the 1960s, I thought the defining American issue was race; however, I gradually realized that racial issues, beginning with slavery, are a result of greed, the truly defining American issue, a base reality as against national claims of high moral purpose. The political climate in 2023 America typified the issue. Indifferent to humanity, Donald Trump fanned racial fires for personal gain and power—it's an ancient, evil dynamic. In contrast, the thread of the whistled, birdlike tune moving through the harsh, bright light and barely holding its own promises the possibility not only of survival but of triumph—restoration, wholeness, joy. Here again Baldwin's lyric gifts are at the fore. The descriptive phrasing of the whistling bird sentence folds somewhat back on itself at each juncture as the line moves forward, producing the sense of sound drifting through the air. The careful, light repetition of *very* helps hold the line together amid contrasts—*complicated/simple, harsh/bright, pouring out/only just holding.* The pattern of consonant and vowel sounds—for instance, *ou* in *pouring, out, though, sound, through,* or

[4] James Baldwin, *The Fire Next Time* (New York: Dell, 1962), 116–17.

the flow of short *i* sounds throughout, with carefully interspersed hard *t, c, p, d, b* and softer consonant notes—provides a quiet, almost prayerful musicality. The feeling in the line is very deep, while the breath is relatively shallow, up in the mouth, on the tongue and lips. The overall effect is of the tune's distinct importance and its tenuousness amid all other confused, indifferent sounds in the city. For the tune to be silenced would be fatal. Sonny, in the midst of his own crisis of identity after the mother's death, lashes out at his brother's ignorance about Charlie Parker. And in all this there's also a subtext or subconscious element of Sonny's attraction to and rationalization for using heroin. Parker, already beginning his rise in the jazz world, was using heroin by the time he was sixteen, just about the age Sonny is at the time of this conversation with his brother.[5] What Sonny couldn't have known then was that Parker would die at the age of thirty-four, the erosion of drugs and alcohol outrunning his sublime gifts. Sonny will experience and come to understand the cost of addiction only much later and, finally, in a kind of torment will reveal it to his brother.

But now the brother lights a cigarette, buying time, surprised to discover that he's trembling. Defensively, he says he's been out of touch and Sonny will have to be patient and explain who Parker is.

Exasperated, Sonny turns his back, and sullenly, bitterly declares Parker's greatness, which, he says, is probably why the brother has never heard of him.

[5] Aaron Olson, "The Connection between Jazz and Drug Abuse: A Comparative Look at the Effects of Widespread Narcotics Abuse on Jazz Music in the 40's, 50's, and 60's," University of Denver, Digital Commons, November 2019, https://digitalcommons.du.edu/cgi/viewcontent.cgi?article=1054&context=musicology_student.

The brother indignantly concedes his ignorance, sarcastically apologizes, and says he'll go out and buy all Parker's records.

Sonny isn't having any of his brother's condescension, doesn't care who he listens to, doesn't want any favors.

The dialogue between the brothers is perfect in tone and pacing, and each character's voice is distinctly individual. The substance of their words does exactly what dialogue should do, which is to provide conflict and characterization. Dialogue is what characters do to each other. It's a sword fight. And in terms of how dialogue creates movement and drama, Jean Cocteau perhaps put it best: The secret is active speech—the chalk line in front of the chicken.[6] If the line isn't there under the words, the spell is broken and the reader won't follow to the end. Each interaction carries the story and its reader forward.

The orphaned brothers are vitally at odds. The older brother has never seen Sonny so upset, and he tells himself it's just something that kids go through, so he shouldn't make it seem so important by pushing it. But he can't quite let it go, and instead he continues with a morally tinged parental attitude, suggesting that it takes a long time to become a musician and asking if Sonny can make a living at it.

Sonny gathers himself, faces his brother, and explains reasonably that everything takes time and, yes, he can makes a living at it, but what he wants his brother to understand is that music is the only thing he wants to do.

The brother gently, reasonably replies that Sonny must know that people can't always do what they want to do.

[6] Jean Cocteau, *The Writer's Life: Intimate Thoughts on Work, Love, Inspiration, and Fame from the Diaries of the World's Great Writers*, ed. Carol Edgarian and Tom Jenks (San Francisco: Narrative Library, 2011), 61.

Sonny surprises him by saying he doesn't know that, and people should do what they want to do, otherwise why are they alive.

The older brother desperately huffs that Sonny's getting to be a big boy and needs to think about his future. Clearly, the older brother would like to get out from under the burden of responsibility and challenge he feels.

Sonny grimly asserts that he thinks about his future all the time. It's a statement grudgingly offered under the circumstances, yet it represents the degree of Sonny's self-possession and desire to take charge of his own life, if he can find a way.

The reader experiences concern for Sonny and sees that both brothers are trying hard in the impasse. Less obvious is that Baldwin is laying the groundwork for a later confrontation between the brothers, in the third act. The brothers' impasse extends across four and half pages, a single long-running scene composed of shorter, constituent movements of conflict, action, and resolution, each movement providing an occasion in which each brother expresses himself to the other relatively bluntly for the first time in their lives, and despite their inability to reconcile their positions and connect, their conversation forms the basis for eventual growth and openness on more familiar terms later.

The extended interaction between Sonny and his brother, like the precursory scene between the brother and the raggy boy, signifies more of Baldwin's skill as a dramatist. Less confident fiction writers tend to whisk their characters on- and offstage, losing tension rather than developing a story toward sustained, escalating interactions in which every drop of dramatic possibility plays itself out within and between the characters. As the reader follows each step of the outer story in "Sonny's Blues," Baldwin also gives access to the inner story, the inner and outer stories playing simultaneously, interpenetrating reciprocally—what happens on the outer plane causing what happens on the inner plane, and vice versa. As narrator, the older brother can relate what was said, what was done, what he thought and felt at the time, what he now knows about it all that he did not know or could not articulate at the time, including elements such as what he thought was going on with Sonny as compared to what turns out to have really been going on with him. The reader lives the story with the characters while having the pleasure of knowing more than they knew moment to moment. And all this is the product of Baldwin's imagination.

How does the storyteller know the story? He knows it by various means. By having lived it, or by having been told it, or by inference from reasonable familiarity with the kinds of events and characters involved, by sympathetic understanding, but finally and most fully by imagination—the faculty by which one knows the things that cannot otherwise be known. The reader doesn't want or need the means of knowing to be explained or rationalized. The reader only needs the storyteller to possess the story and to tell it well. Flannery O'Connor noted that an author must be able to dominate the world he creates.[7] *Dominate* may be misleading, seeming to imply an overbearing power, but O'Connor meant an overarching godlike ability to create. The successful author is the authority for the work and for every detail in it—authority not in the sense of power to enforce obedience but authority as in its Latin root, *originate*. And as with storytelling, so with music making. By the end of "Sonny's Blues" Baldwin will have fully dramatized a correspondence between the two art forms.

[7] O'Connor, *Habit of Being*, 106.

Confronted by Sonny's intractability over music, the older brother gives up, deciding they can talk about it later and reminding Sonny that he has to finish school and will be moving in with the brother's wife Isabel and her parents while the older brother is away in the army.

Sonny doesn't respond right away. He moves from the kitchen table to the window. Windows are recurrent images in the story. As literal details, the windows are part of the physical description and stage blocking in the story—characters move to and from them, look out and away from them—and thus the windows constitute part of the increasingly familiar pathway or plot of the story. As metaphors—portals of vision—they are occasions of perception and perspective, greater or lesser degrees of clarity, nearer or more distant approaches to truth on the part of the character or characters at a window. Each character tries to see a way forward, succeeding or failing by increments in relation to and in conflict with self and others. The use of perspective—the interplay between each character's view, along with the narrator's view as distinct from the characters' views—provides the reader with the accurate relationship between all things.

Sonny finally says that moving to Isabel's is a terrible idea and that his brother knows it.

The brother asks if Sonny has a better idea. It's a rhetorical question that seems to corner Sonny.

He paces in the kitchen. The brother notices Sonny has grown as tall as him and has started to shave. The older brother suddenly feels he doesn't know Sonny at all.

Sonny picks up the brother's pack of cigarettes, and an escalating emotional contest ensues, in which Sonny mockingly asks permission to smoke, the brother thinks he's still too young, and

Sonny lights up, saying he wanted to see if he had the courage to smoke in front of his brother, and it was easy. He says he bets the brother was smoking when he was Sonny's age. The brother can't deny it, and something strained comes into Sonny's laugh as he says he bets smoking wasn't all the brother was doing.

All this frightens the brother and he tries to cut off Sonny's mockery, insisting again that they've already decided on Sonny moving in with Isabel and her parents.

Sonny accusingly says that the brother decided it. Sonny leans against the stove, his arms loosely folded, and earnestly says he doesn't want to stay in Harlem anymore. He looks toward the window, and the brother registers worry in Sonny's eyes. Then Sonny rubs the muscle of one arm.

The gesture is a tell that in the moment the brother misses and that the reader may also miss. Sonny physically manifests the thing that he cannot bring himself to say. He's approximately touching the crook of his arm where he would shoot up, and, whether consciously or semiconsciously, he's indicating in this sideways manner why he needs to get out of Harlem and the weight of pain, shame, and fear he feels. This sort of occluded or partially disguised confession is so very lifelike and frequently occurs when someone wants to be relieved of a secret that holds them apart from others and the open flow of life.

The brother asks Sonny where he wants to go. And though Sonny is underage, he says he wants to join the army or navy—he thinks that if he says he's old enough, they'll believe him. The brother reacts angrily, in fear for Sonny's life. Baldwin doesn't specify the exact date of the events of the story, but the backstory in Act II when Sonny is still in high school takes place two or three years after the boys' father's death in the middle of

World War II. The mother's death happens when Charlie Parker is still alive and at the height of his fame. He died in 1955, so the approximate time period when Sonny wants to enlist seems to be between the mid to late 1940s and the Korean War (1950–1953), when life-and-death jeopardy attended military service, thus the older brother's concern for Sonny's safety.

The older brother again emphasizes Sonny's need to finish school and rather desperately asks how Sonny's going to study music if he's in the army.

Sonny says he'll work something out, and he'll have the G.I. Bill when he's done serving.

The brother pleads with him. Sonny says he's not learning anything in school, even when he does go. He turns away from his brother, opens the window, and tosses his cigarette into the alley. It's a *narrow* alley—the adjective making a subtle metaphoric correspondence to Sonny's limited possibilities of choice. The pacing of the scene from the time Sonny lights the cigarette to his tossing it out is exactly right for the time it would take him to smoke the cigarette, and the gesture of tossing it reinforces a sense of futility. He says he's not learning anything in school that the brother would want him to learn anyway, and then he slams the window shut, angrily and with a connotation of foreclosure on his life.

The brother's plea grows fervent. He says he knows how Sonny feels, and if he quits school, he'll be sorry later. The brother grabs Sonny's shoulders, reasoning with him, and then swears that if Sonny will finish his last year of school, the brother will help Sonny do whatever he wants to do, once the brother comes home from the army. Please, do that for me, the brother pleads.

Sonny doesn't answer and won't look at his brother.

The brother implores Sonny to listen. Sonny pulls away and says that he hears the brother but that the brother never hears what Sonny has to say.

The brother doesn't know what to say. Sonny looks out the window and then back at the brother and finally agrees to try to finish school.

Then, to cheer Sonny up, the brother says there's a piano at Isabel's and Sonny can practice on it.

The thought does cheer Sonny up. He relaxes a bit but shadows of worry play on his face as if he is staring into a fire.

Still in backstory, following a line space, Baldwin moves forward in time, covering what happens with Sonny while the brother is away in the army and immediately after he comes back from service. In summary narration that plays palpably as direct drama, the older brother describes Sonny at Isabel's, practicing the piano, playing a chord, a change, a progression over and over, incessantly. The sound doesn't make any sense to Isabel and her parents. For them, living with Sonny is like living with a god, or a monster. Reading this section of "Sonny's Blues," I'm reminded again of John Coltrane. After serving in the navy in Hawaii, where he played saxophone with a navy swing band, he lived in Philadelphia in his sister's house. He was excited about jazz and learned all the sheet music for the saxophone, and then still using the saxophone he learned the sheet music for the other wind instruments. At night when his sister's household was asleep, Coltrane would sit in the dark on a chair in the dining room and practice the fingerings on the sax without blowing, as he didn't want to disturb the house. He was putting in the work required to develop artistry. About learning to play, Charlie Parker recalled, "I put quite a bit of study into the horn. In fact, the neighbors threatened to ask my mother to move once, you know."[8] There's a saying from Lao-tzu, the sixth-century author of the *Tao Te Ching*: "Those who say don't know, and those who know don't say." This thought has sometimes been applied to jazz and other arts, with a sense that deft performance is more a matter of instinctive gifts than of practice and acquired skill. This interpretation of the saying encourages the idea that thinking and talking about the art may take the life out of it, or, in other words, that art rises from the unconscious self and thinking about the art will kill it. But since the unconscious is infinite and the conscious self can never fully encompass it, the more conscious the artist is about his or her work, up to a point, the more opportunity and ability he or she has to draw inspiration from the reservoir of the unconscious. It's important to know on what level to understand things. There are examples of spontaneous acts of mastery or genius, such as in Coleridge's fragmentary "Kubla Khan," though these instances are few and far between and generally come from artists who have already attained mastery. Musicians with Coltrane's chops and writers at Baldwin's level have habituated their skills, just as a great baseball hitter, like Ted Williams, practiced his swing many times daily across his career and studied the swings of others and the delivery of pitchers, so that with mastered skills, improvisation can occur at the fingertips, as if without thought. Magicians are known to say, *There's nothing in my hand*. Of course, there's something in the hand, but the words and gestures obscure how

[8] Charlie Parker, https://www.brainyquote.com/authors/charlie-parker-quotes.

the trick is done. The audience is not meant to see all the labor but to have the benefit of it. Yeats put it this way in his poem "Adam's Curse":

> A line will take us hours maybe;
> Yet if it does not seem a moment's thought,
> Our stitching and unstitching has been naught.[9]

While giving a dazzling performance in "Sonny's Blues," Baldwin lets the reader see some of what can be required in order to have any hope of summoning such a performance—Sonny as a man/child, practicing his art on faith, playing for his life, while Isabel and her family try to take care of him in the ordinary ways of shelter, food, and conventional expectations, all the while enduring the unfamiliar, inharmonious, seemingly chaotic, repetitive sounds he's making, day and night. He's polite but wrapped up in the music, and unreachable. His brother, thousands of miles away, reading Isabel's letters, senses what's going on at home, but what can he do?

Meanwhile, Sonny's been skipping school. Isabel's mother receives a letter from the school board, and it turns out there'd been earlier letters that Sonny intercepted and tore up. A confrontation ensues, and Isabel's mother finally gets Sonny to confess that he's been hanging out in Greenwich Village with other musicians at a white girl's apartment. Scared by this news, Isabel's mother screams at Sonny about all the sacrifices made for him and how little he appreciates any of it.

Sonny doesn't play the piano that day. Isabel's mother calms down, but then Isabel's father reprimands him, and Isabel starts crying. Sonny feels what Isabel and her parents are feeling, and

[9] William Butler Yeats, *W. B. Yeats*, ed. Seamus Heany (London: Faber & Faber, 2019), 18.

the older brother narrates that even had they been gentler than people are ordinarily capable of being, Sonny is bound to feel as if they have stripped him naked and are spitting on him. He sees that his music, which is life or death for him, has been a torture for them and that they have endured it not for his sake but for that of the older brother, and Sonny can't take that. Baldwin writes, "He can take it a little better today than he could then, but he's still not very good at it and, frankly, I don't know anybody who is." As in Act I, with the use of the present tense in describing the housing project where the older brother lives, here Baldwin's use of the present tense indicates the relationship in time between the events of the story and the moment of their telling. The reader is given an indication that things with Sonny will improve somewhat, but his struggle is not over, nor would it be for anyone made to feel shame for no other reason than existing. And music, as a subject and medium of the story, makes Sonny's aspiration as universal as it is particular to him and his race.

The older brother conjectures that the silence in the household over the next few days must have been louder than all the music ever played since the world began. Then, one morning before work, Isabel looks into Sonny's room, and he's cleared out. He's joined the navy and disappeared other than for a postcard eventually mailed home from Greece. Some years pass until both Sonny and his brother are out of the service and back in New York.

Sonny's a man now, but the brother won't accept it. He disapproves of how Sonny carries himself, doesn't like Sonny's friends, considers his music an excuse for living a louche, disordered life. The brothers argue and stay away from each other for months. Then one day the brother wants to make up with Sonny and goes to see him in the furnished room where he's living in the Village. But there are a lot of people in the room, Sonny's lying on the bed, won't get up, treats the other people like they're his family, and the brother loses his temper. He tells Sonny that he's as good as dead, living the way he does, and Sonny stands up and says not to worry about him because he *is* dead where the brother is concerned. Sonny pushes the brother out and slams the door, behind which the brother hears laughter. Tears come to his eyes, and to keep from crying he starts whistling, vindictively holding a self-pitying thought that Sonny's going to need him one of these days. The hopeful birdlike whistling from earlier in the story darkens to a dirge. The pathos is real even as the brother indulges himself in his sense of his own rightness. But in narrating what he did and did not do, he vulnerably shows himself, flaws and all.

As a narrator, the older brother gives the reader a perspective from which to see him more objectively than he could view himself at the time of the events and from which to judge fairly, according to the reader's own lights. Every individual experiences life unfolding on the basis of his or her own existence. Consequently, every individual has the conviction of his or her own illusions, and characters in fiction must be allowed their illusions, too. This is a subtle business: on the one hand, Baldwin writes the story so that it welcomes the reader's unconscious projective identifications and shows the characters as self-justified, thus allowing them their illusions and fallacies, and on the other, he reveals the error of those fallacies, indicates better choices, and confronts the reader's assumptions, without, however, insulting the reader or breaking the tissue of the fiction by being heavy-handed or severely undercutting.

Act II ends with the rupture between the brothers, followed by a line space, indicating another jump in time and circumstance.

ACT III

Some years have passed, and the narrator relates that he'd read about Sonny's arrest in the spring, and so the reader is back in the front story that started at the top of the first page with the older brother's subway ride to work. Now the story moves steadily forward in time to the ending, with the exception of a half page of backstory concerning the death of the older brother's beautiful two-year-old daughter, Grace. She'd had a fever for a couple of days, and then it dropped, and she seemed fine. Then one day she was playing, and Isabel, who was fixing lunch in the kitchen, heard Grace fall in the living room. She didn't scream or call out, and the fall might have been nothing serious, but when Isabel heard the thump of the fall and then silence, she felt afraid and raced to the living room. Grace was on the floor, struggling to get her breath, her body contorted by an attack of polio. She screamed, and in the older brother's telling, as with his mother's telling of the flying strings of the busted guitar earlier in the story, Grace's scream and, before it, the thump of her falling have a mortal impact that pierces the reader. The sounds convey the feelings. Baldwin never strains to create an emotional response. He writes clearly and precisely. Any heightening or flourishing of language to produce effects would be unconvincing, because it would preempt the reader's engagement. Dispassionate writing allows the reader's emotions to enter the story. As Chekhov noted, "When you want to touch the reader's heart, try to be colder. It gives their grief, as it were, a background against which it stands out in great relief."[1]

In the present-time of the telling of the story—that is, in the ongoing lives of the characters from beyond the end of the story—Isabel continues to suffer and mourn the loss of her child, sometimes waking the older brother up with her moans. He holds her, and where she weeps against him seems an open wound. Such sorrow and efforts at comfort between husband and wife call on the compassion of any reader. As Baldwin intends, each step in the story deepens the felt experience and has a quickening, humanizing effect on the reader.

The daughter's name signifies absolutely. Literally, Grace has died. Metaphorically, life's blessing disappears.

The older brother remembers that on the day of Grace's burial, his grief prompted him finally to write to Sonny in jail (the letter and the brothers' reunion on Sonny's release having previously been narrated in Act I). Here, at the start of Act III, Baldwin touches on it all again as the story approaches a culmination in the opening out of vulnerability and sustained engagement between the brothers.

Sonny's been out of prison and living with the brother and Isabel for two weeks, and the older brother, who is home alone for a little while, finds himself restlessly wandering about the apartment, drinking a beer, while trying to summon the courage to search Sonny's room for drugs. The older brother stands at the living room window, looking out on Seventh Avenue. The

[1] V. S. Pritchett, *Chekhov: A Spirit Set Free* (New York: Random House, 1988), 116.

images *living room* and *window* are important, consistent elements in Baldwin's plot design and pattern of meaning. There are numerous ways to read a story—for the simple enjoyment of the story, of course, which is the primary and intended way for general readers. But for a reader wanting to know more about how the story was made, how it works its magic, other ways of readings are revealing. For instance, a story can be read with singular focus on its dramatic structure (plot), scene by scene, and how each scene is constructed, beginning, middle, and end, and within each scene how the characters' conflicts are deployed, and from scene to scene how the transitions are achieved. Or a story can be read with attention, phrase by phrase, line by line, to the author's use of point of view, what work it does, how it's done, what differences can be discerned between the narrator's view and that of the characters, and what's moving perceptually within and between the characters. Or a story can be read for the author's means of characterization, posed as it always must be between body and soul, physicality providing a correlative to the condition of the soul, which in turn determines a character's fate. And, among many other ways of reading a story, descriptions, sensory details, and patterns of imagery can be tracked to see what they may reveal beyond the literal tapestry of life often taken for granted and, in a story, not overtly calling attention to their effects but naturalistically present. The setting of "Sonny's Blues" is domestic and confined—the workaday commute on the subway, the cab ride uptown, the neighborhood, the home with its familiar rooms, furnishings, and outlooks onto the street scene. Harlem, yes, a very specific and distinct place, yet Baldwin's handling of the setting evokes ordinary homes everywhere. The persistence of certain images—*window, face, bird, living room, kitchen, light, piano,* for instance—have a unifying, orienting, often consoling effect in a tangible world that can be counted on. Other images—*ice, darkness, shadow, heroin*—carry a counterbalance of dread. And some of the images in the long run of the story cut both ways, depending on the moment and how the image is modified and cast—for instance, *naked,* as in Sonny's adolescent dreams of pilgrimage to India, or *naked* as in Sonny's feeling of being exposed and reviled by Isabel and her parents. The dramatic movement of the story gradually, gracefully transforms the images in a totality of effects that express Baldwin's intended meaning.

Standing indecisively at the window, not knowing what he'll do if he finds drugs or if he doesn't, the brother looks down on the street, where a corner revival meeting is going on. A few people are gathered. A barbecue cook stands in a doorway, smoking a cigarette, watching. Kids and some older men are paused, watching, along with some tough-looking women who habitually watch the street as though they own it, or perhaps are owned by it. Three sisters in Black and a brother are holding the revival, and they flourish their voices, Bibles, and a tambourine. The brother testifies, and the sisters utter *amens* and hold out the tambourine for coins, which one sister pockets. Then she raises her hands, shakes the tambourine in the air, and she and the other three begin to sing "Tis' the Old Ship of Zion." The hymn dates from the late nineteenth century and was derived from earlier spiritual and gospel lyrics. The song promises that the ship will carry its voyagers over the difficult waters to a brighter destination—many a thousand will be rescued. The brother, like everyone else in Harlem, has seen street revivals all his life, but now it seems strange to him. He narrates:

> Not a soul under the sound of their voices was hearing this song for the first time, not a one of them had been rescued. Nor had they seen much in the way of rescue work being done around them. Neither did they especially believe in the holiness of the three sisters and the brother, they knew too much about them, knew where they lived, and how.

In *The Fire Next Time,* Baldwin records the evolution of his faith:

> The church was very exciting. It took a long time for me to disengage myself from this excitement, and on the blindest, most visceral level, I never really have, and never will. There is no music like that music, no drama like the drama of the saints rejoicing, the sinners moaning, the tambourines racing, and all those voices coming together and crying holy unto the Lord. There is still, for me, no pathos quite like the pathos of those multicolored, worn, somehow triumphant and transfigured faces, speaking from the depths of a visible, tangible, continuing despair of the goodness of the Lord...
>
> I date it—the slow crumbling of my faith, the pulverization of my fortress—from the time, about a year after I had begun to preach...
>
> Being in the pulpit was like being in the theatre; I was behind the scenes and knew how the illusion was worked.... I knew how to work on a congregation until the last dime was surrendered—it was not very hard to do—and I knew where the money for "the Lord's work" went.
>
> ... when I faced a congregation, it began to take all the strength I had not to stammer, not to curse, not to tell them to throw away their Bibles and get off their knees and go home and organize, for example, a rent strike. When I watched all the children, their copper, brown, and beige faces staring up at me as I taught Sunday school, I felt that I was committing a crime in talking about the gentle Jesus, in telling them to reconcile themselves to their misery on earth in order to gain the crown of eternal life....

> I had been in the pulpit too long and I had seen too many monstrous things. I don't refer merely to the glaring fact that the minister eventually acquires houses and Cadillacs while the faithful continue to scrub floors and drop their dimes and quarters and dollars into the plate. I really mean that there was no love in the church. It was a mask for hatred and self-hatred and despair. The transfiguring power of the Holy Ghost ended when the service ended, and salvation stopped at the church door. When we were told to love everybody, I had thought that that meant *every body*. But no. It applied only to those who believed as we did, and it did not apply to white people at all.[2]

Baldwin soon left off preaching and turned to writing. He came to believe that religion would not suffice to create needed change. By writing he could do more.

Organized religion tends to put myth into a fixed, ritualized, unchanging pattern rather than allowing myth to progress, whereas storytelling involves a continual reimagining and reinterpretation of life's meanings as time and generations advance. Myths say the things about life that cannot otherwise be said, or not as well said and shown. Poets and writers get there first—before the theologians. Bible stories, creation stories, and other stories passed down in modern religions, including stories of the origins and names of gods, are based on and adapted from ancient myths. The moments in which the older brother stands at the window looking out at the revival offer a pause that marks a perceptual shift both personal (to the older brother and to Baldwin) and societal, in the flow of collective mystical participation by which human needs and instincts take shape in the world. Throughout "Sonny's Blues," Baldwin reimagines and

[2] Baldwin, *Fire Next Time*, 49–58.

reinterprets the myths that preceded him. The myth of Cain and Abel, for instance, or of one person's superiority over another by fact of race, or the myth that a person can dehumanize another person without in turn being dehumanized. The pause and perceptual shift at the window announce a crucial turning point about to come in the story.

In the pause, the older brother starkly observes the conflicted nature of Harlem—the confluence of innocence and experience, of paradise and hell, in the face of a battered woman with darkly glittering eyes watching a woman singing brightly, in the gesture of the barbecue cook indifferently dropping his cigarette and another man fumbling impatiently for coins to drop into the tambourine and looking furious about it.

Then the brother sees Sonny in the crowd, looking like a schoolboy, smiling and coppery in the sun. He drops coins into the tambourine and starts toward home. For the first time the older brother notices that Sonny has a loping walk, with his own half-beat, a kind of hipster walk, and the reader receives a quick image of Sonny's inner music.

When Sonny gets home the brother is relieved to see him and apprehensive, too, but offers him a beer, a big gesture, given how worried the brother is about drugs. Throughout the piece, there's an implicit representation of the relationship between the numbing effects of heroin and of alcohol and the dangers involved. Sonny at first declines. He joins his brother at the window and remarks on the warmth of a voice singing "If Only I Could Hear My Mother Pray Again," a gospel lament celebrating a mother's Christian virtues and her grown child's desire for return to childhood faith. The older brother agrees about the warmth of the voice and quips that she sure can beat that tambourine.

"But what a terrible song," Sonny replies and laughs. Here Baldwin brings a touch of humor and lightness to the darkness and dread and indicates the inadequacy or impossibility of regressing to childhood faith, given adult realities. Sonny's a man now. His laughter over the somber gospel song sounds softer, milder, more mature than was his angry teenage dismissal of Louis Armstrong yet strikes further notes in a generational musical progression from spirituals to blues to jazz. Music, myth, and man are advancing together.

Sonny goes to the kitchen and returns with a beer, an acceptance of his brother's offer and a slight lowering of the fears separating them. The offer and acceptance of the beer, along with the passage of time and event, maturation and rapprochement, have created an opening. And Sonny invites his brother to go somewhere with him that night. The brother senses that he can't say no, agrees to go, and then asks where.

Sonny sits down on the sofa, picks up a notebook, and leafs through it, shy motions of indirection, given the brothers' past conflicts over music and Sonny's uncertainty of the outcome between them, but he finally confides that he's going to play with a group in the Village.

The brother responds with a sense of wonder at the news that Sonny's going to play. Sonny confirms it, sips his beer, moves to the window, and looking sidelong at his brother, says, "If you can stand it."

The brother says he'll try.

Baldwin touches the moment with humor and irony, and in each small gesture between the brothers, there's an inch of courage. As distinct from physical boldness or bravery, courage is at the heart—the proactive willingness to be emotionally vulnerable and open. Throughout "Sonny's Blues," the reader is in touch with the characters' hearts because Baldwin shares his heart with the reader. This quality impressed Maya Angelou, who noted:

> I continue to see not only his craftsmanship but his courage. That means a lot to me. Courage may be the most important of all the virtues because without it one cannot practice any other virtues with consistency.[3]

And as always when human connection is of vital importance and the possibility of achieving it has been limited or constrained, a small movement in a positive direction, or the opposite, can produce a strong sympathetic response in the reader. The smaller the possibility, the greater the magnitude of the response in relation to the desired outcome—in this case the desire that the brothers will overcome what divides them.

They watch the revival meeting breaking up. The three sisters and the brother are singing "God Be with You Till We Meet Again." Baldwin provides no comment on the hymn, and the reader need not give it a thought while caught up in the story; however, Baldwin's choice of the hymn expresses meaning. The word *goodbye* is a sixteenth-century British contraction of *God be with ye,* a phrase from the late fourteenth century. Throughout time the word *good* has often been substituted for the word *God,* making the association *God is good.* The hymn title, which is the hymn's salient, repeated line, invokes providence (God's goodness) on the occasion of people parting from each other with the promise of

[3] Maya Angelou, interview, *Black Women Writers,* 11.

meeting again. The hymn implies shared belief in providence and in a meeting in the next life, if not this one. When the brothers' mother, whose faith was deep, counseled the older brother always to be there for Sonny, she would have been thinking of her sons' mortal and immortal fate. Without a redeeming connection in this life, could there be one in the next? The thread of "Sonny's Blues" follows the fate of two individuals parting and meeting, within a larger context of races divided from one another. More so than the earlier referenced spirituals "Lord, You Brought Me from a Long Ways Off," "Tis' the Old Ship of Zion," and "If Only I Could Hear My Mother Pray Again," the hymn "God Be with You Till We Meet Again" would have been familiar to white readers. The hymn was written in 1882 by Jeremiah Rankin, a white clergyman, an abolitionist who became the sixth president of Howard University, which was founded shortly after the Civil War as a Black college and university. In its first five years the school educated more than 150,000 freed slaves. Later Rankin's hymn was adapted and printed on postcards given as a consoling encouragement to soldiers going into battle in World War I. Originally penned for a Congregationalist church choir and scored by William Toomer, a musical director at a Methodist Episcopal church, the hymn appears in Baptist, Mormon, and other denominational hymnals. Baldwin would have known all, or much, of this background. He posits the song as an image of one people, one destiny, undivided. Listening to the hymn, the street crowd grows quiet with reverence. The song ends, the crowd disperses.

Sonny abruptly remarks that the sound of the woman singing reminded him of what heroin made him feel like—warm, cool, distant, and in control. He sips his beer and avoids looking at his brother, but he's taken a big step, directly voicing the fearsome unspoken thing between them. He says that sometimes you have to have that feeling. The way he says it, using the second-person *you*, objectifies it, as if it's outside of him.

The brother pins Sonny, skeptically asking, "Do you?" Then the older brother sits slowly down in an *easy chair*, an image recurring from Act II, and it's as if the backstory scene when the children listened to the old folks talking quietly as night came on has advanced to the point that the children have become the adults. The older brother's braced against opening up to what he's long avoided knowing, though his part of the conversation, which mainly calls on him to be receptive, is easier than Sonny's, which requires making a clean breast of things. From the story's beginning, the narration is the older brother's confession, within which now Sonny undertakes his own confession. He responds elliptically that sometimes some people need that drugged feeling.

The older brother angrily, contemptuously asks if it's needed in order to play music.

Sonny looks at his brother with troubled eyes, as if his look can communicate what he can't bear to say, and then he responds that *they* think they need it, and if they think—

The brother interrupts like an inquisitor, asking what Sonny thinks.

Sonny sits on the sofa and puts his beer can on the floor. He says he doesn't know and seems to get lost in his own thoughts. Then he says taking the drug is not so much about playing but about being able to withstand life, to keep from falling apart.

The brother harshly suggests that Sonny's friends fall apart damn fast anyway.

Sonny doesn't agree or disagree. He says maybe. He fiddles with his notebook. His brother senses that he should be quiet and listen, because Sonny is trying hard to explain himself. Here the older brother makes a considerable advance by refraining from judgment, and his restraint reciprocates Sonny's vulnerability in having started the conversation.

Sonny takes the opening provided by his brother's softened attitude and mildly argues that some people don't fall apart or haven't yet and that's about all anyone can say. He pauses and then admits that some people live in hell, knowing that they do, and they keep taking the drug anyway. "I don't know," Sonny says, and with that line, Baldwin gives an echo of the older brother's characteristic denials—not wanting to know—but the words in Sonny's mouth are an honest effort, a moment-to-moment struggle to express himself and the truth he wants his brother to know. Sonny sighs, drops his notebook, folds his arms, and haltingly explains that some musicians he knows are on drugs all the time and they want to be, even if they say they don't.

The older brother asks specifically about Sonny—what he wants.

Sonny gets up, walks to the window, and stands silently for a long time. He sighs. All the characters' gestures, pacing, and dialogue in the scene convey sublimated pain. Sonny says, "Me," both an acknowledgment and dismissal of himself—the problem being very personal yet involving so much more than a single soul. He says that while he was listening to the sister sing, it struck him how much suffering she went through to sing like that, and it's repulsive to think anyone has to suffer that much.

The older brother counters rhetorically that there's no way not to suffer, is there?

Sonny smiles mockingly and agrees, pointedly adding that the fact of suffering hasn't kept anyone from trying to avoid it. This jab begins to bring home to the older brother how unforgivably he has failed at helping Sonny.

Earlier in the story, the older brother related that Sonny isn't talkative; however, at each juncture between the brothers, Sonny has tried to talk, and now the older brother, in the working out of his confession, recognizes that he has withheld himself when Sonny most needed him. Part of the miracle of "Sonny's Blues" is that the occasion of the telling is the older brother's gradual arrival at the meaning of all that's happened. The reader experiences and participates in his growth of consciousness. Crucially, in Act III, Sonny emerges as an articulate truth teller, and the truths are hard to speak and hard to hear. He turns back to the window and says bitterly that suffering is a given, yet *you* try not to drown in it, to stay on top of it, and to make it seem like you did something to deserve suffering. Sonny pushes the argument at his brother, who stays silent. Sonny persists, emphasizing the unreasonableness of suffering and concluding, "Maybe it's better . . . to give it a reason, *any* reason."

The older brother doesn't want to hear this and argues that since suffering is a given, it's better just to take it.

Sonny denies it and heatedly observes that nobody just takes it and that the brother simply prefers his own way of avoiding suffering.

Sonny is penetrating the core of his brother's defenses, and the brother strongly rejects Sonny's characterization and adds that he doesn't care what other people do, how they suffer, he cares only how Sonny suffers. Sonny watches his brother closely, and the brother continues that he doesn't want Sonny to die trying to avoid suffering.

Sonny responds flatly that he won't die that way and not faster than anyone else.

Still unwilling to be convinced, the older brother laughs uneasily and reasons that there's no need in killing yourself, as if it were a question.

The dispute has reached a high pitch. The older brother wants to say more but can't. He's thinking about willpower, and how life can be beautiful, and how everything is within. Or is it? he wonders. Or isn't that the problem? He wants to promise Sonny not to fail him again, but saying so seems dishonest to him. So instead he promises himself not to fail and prays that he can keep the promise. This huge shift in him has come about not all at once but by virtue of myriad small steps forward and backward and forward again, compelled by unavoidable circumstance (beginning with the news of Sonny's arrest) and by time—that is, mortality, by which I mean not simply the specter of death but the force that finite time exerts on all people. Life is movement and metamorphosis. People either choose and accept necessary change or refuse it. Those who resist change are nonetheless altered, and not for the better, by changes that occur all around them and act on them and by time, the great mover of life (and of story). In "Sonny's Blues" and other stories with a moral dimension and concerning the inevitability of human error, characters' choices fundamentally engage the reader's attention to right and wrong action. Typically, characters, not unlike people in real life, may be any of the following: lost, deluded, misled, mistaken, in the dark, obstinate, corrupt, degraded, vain, petty, selfish, irascible, mean, cowardly, conniving. These conditions and other human failings make for good drama, and in the hands of an accomplished author, the worse a character's traits and behaviors, and the more inimical the overall conditions of a life, ironically, the more the reader may pull for a restorative outcome. The concept of right action presupposes the existence of innate morality combined with moral imagination—the former being a compass, the latter prompting active steps on a correct path. Persons, characters, will make mistakes. They will question and reason. What would, or should, I do? The natural desire is to correct mistakes, to get things right—and not tomorrow, not next week or next year, but now. Distractions, rationalizations, missteps abound, but the clock is running, time grows short, broken situations can worsen, and soon it's too late to alter them—a subject for tragedy. "Sonny's Blues" partakes of individual and societal tragedy while pursuing healing. Societal betterment depends on individual betterment, so Baldwin bases the story on individual characters' lives to engage as many individual readers as possible. As the youngest character in the story, Sonny has by definition the most possibility, and as the ex-convict, the addict who's clean, and as the artist, Sonny has the most to prove, the most at stake, the most urgency in a narrow world—urgency because of the continuing threat of addiction and because of his talent, his need to fulfill it and achieve self-expression, especially with all he's put into becoming a musician.

Almost as if reading his brother's mind—and how very familiar Sonny would be with how his brother thinks and talks to himself from how he talks to Sonny, and he would instantly recognize the hesitating disbelief in his brother's silence—Sonny says that the inner life is terrible sometimes. He's talking about his own experience, but he might as well be talking about the deep core of his brother's denied experience, too. Without a trace of self-pity Sonny describes what it's been like for him to be a Black man—alienated, nowhere to turn, no one to talk to, nothing to do, and no way to relieve the horrible tumult inside—he can't make love with it, and whenever he finally gets with it to play music, it's as if no one listens, so he tries to listen.

Then he walks away from the window and sits on the sofa again, as if the wind's been knocked out of him. He talks about the extremity of needing to play, of being willing to do anything to play, of being willing to cut his mother's throat—he laughs and looks at his brother—or his brother's throat—Sonny sobers—or his own throat. He reassuringly says he's all right now, he thinks he'll be all right, but he can't forget where and what he's been.

The brother asks what Sonny has been.

Sonny smiles, sitting sideways, lounging on the sofa, his fingers playing across his face, as he avoids looking at this brother. He says he's been something he didn't recognize, didn't know he could be, didn't know anybody could be. He pauses, going inward, looking helpless and conflicted. He says he's talking about it now not because he feels guilty, though it might be better if he did, he doesn't know, but he can't really talk about it to anyone. He turns to face his brother and explains that when he was most out of it, he felt most with it and could play—it just came out of him—but thinking about it he doesn't know how he played and he recognizes that during those times he did terrible things to people, because to him they weren't real. He picks up his beer can, and it's empty. Metaphorically, it's as if he's had his fix and has come to the end of what it can do for him, if not to the end of wanting. He goes on to say that at times he needed a fix in order to find a space to listen but he couldn't find it and went crazy, doing terrible things to himself. He doesn't literalize or specify what terrible things were done, and the reader infers the withering physical, emotional, and spiritual toll of heroin addiction. He presses the beer can between his hands. The metal begins to give, glinting like a knife, and the brother's afraid that Sonny will cut himself, but he doesn't interrupt. And Sonny reveals the abject confusion and near inhumanity of where he's been, sweating, crying, shaking, smelling his own stink, thinking he would die if he couldn't get away from the stink while knowing that everything he was doing was locking him in it. He says he didn't know—he continues flattening the beer can—and still doesn't know, yet something told him that maybe it was good to smell his own stink, though he hadn't thought that that was what he was trying to do. Sonny drops the ruined beer can, as empty and ruined as he'd been on smack. The gesture of dropping the empty can offers a resonance and allusion to the biblical image of draining a cup. Ambivalent in its import, the image conveys contradictory possibilities of blessing or damnation, the outcome depending on human choice and action. Provided as descriptive detail embodying Sonny's struggle, the image will come more tellingly into play at the end of the story. Sonny gives his brother a small, fixed smile and goes back to the window as if it is a touchstone. In terms of perception and the chance for connection wrought by confession, the window emblemizes Sonny's hard-won, tenuous self-possession as well as a barrier remaining between him and all he needs and wants. The brother watches Sonny, while Sonny watches the avenue, much as his mother used to watch it, worrying about him. Sonny says that what he could not tell the brother when their mother died and the reason that he wanted to leave Harlem was that he wanted to get away from drugs. Earlier, in the second-act scene between the brothers after the mother's death, the reader witnessed Sonny's turmoil and his struggle to communicate by gesture (touching his inner arm), the peril he felt but could not bring himself to say, all of which for the reader lends greater reality and emotional consequence to his confessing it now.

He goes on to say that what he ran away from was still there when he returned, and that he hadn't changed, he was only older. He falls silent, drumming his fingers on the window pane.

The sun has set, night is coming on. The brother watches Sonny's face. "It can come again," Sonny says, almost to himself, and turning to his brother, Sonny repeats it, because he wants his brother to know.

The older brother absorbs this news and after a pause of shock says, "All right. So it can come again. All right."

Sonny smiles sorrowfully, not masking the awfulness he's imparted, and says, "I had to try to tell you."

The brother responds that yes, he understands.

"You're my brother," Sonny says, looking straight at his brother and not smiling.

The brother repeats that yes, he understands. As in the old church song their mother hummed toward the end of her life, Sonny and his brother have been brought from a long ways off.

Denial has fallen away, and accepting Sonny's truth, the brother accepts himself as well.

In these movements between the brothers, Baldwin presents the reality that in human lives nothing proceeds other than in relationship. A person, or character, may arrive at a recognition or perceive a truth and decide to follow the new awareness to mend or alter thought and behavior, but until the resolution is put into play and tested in relation to other people, it's not proven or earned. Commonly in life, a person's inner determinations are quickly challenged by the vicissitudes of outer life. Credible storytelling mirrors this phenomenon. The older brother's decision to keep quiet and listen faces Sonny's hard-to-hear struggle to impart his anguish. Ultimately, having received Sonny's utterance, the older brother is further called on to make a response that entirely departs from his lifelong manner of understanding himself and his brother. Meanwhile, Sonny, having reached the bottom of himself and striving to rise, finds for the first time frank words about his past and honestly expresses his intent and uncertainty about maintaining sobriety.

The brothers connect. Their reunion alters and strengthens each brother, a communion their mother understood and urged, though in her devotion to containing her husband's ever-present pain from the past and to helping protect their sons from harsh knowledge of Black life in white America, she could protect them only so much and could not help participating in creating a condition of denial in the older brother and a desire for escape in Sonny.

Baldwin depicts human nature and all other aspects of "Sonny's Blues" with complete integrity, a unity of elements. The break between the brothers began in Sonny's adolescence (when he dreamed of going to India), when childhood innocence and unknowing gave way, in the language of the story, to *knowing too much too soon about what would happen to him* and when the older brother was already embedded in denial with an edge of the father's stance of superiority and imperviousness. The brothers' reunion occurs only after every alternative has been exhausted, short of final disconnection and death. The story arrives at the short, quarter-page culmination of reunion after a six-page dramatic buildup from the opening of Act III, with the older brother looking out the window at the street revival, the equivocal aspiration of which contrasts, in the playing out of the scene, with the fulfilled reunion, or revived brotherhood. Notably, Baldwin composes the culmination in perfectly paced and modulated short lines of dialogue, each carrying full weight of accumulated meaning. Simplicity is the stamp of truth. Baldwin's use of that principle, after everything else that has occurred and has been said between the brothers, produces a powerful, shimmeringly tender emotional effect. A reader would have to be made of stone not to feel and accord to the trembling heart in Sonny's words *You're my brother* and his brother answering *Yes, I understand.*

So strong and complete is the moment that a lesser writer might start to tie up the ending here. After all, the brothers are reunited, the promise and desire offered the reader in the beginning to bring the estranged brothers together and show what happens has been fulfilled. But Baldwin's not a whit sentimental and doesn't rest on the reunion. Sonny turns back to the window, looks out, and says, "All that hatred down there, all that hatred, misery, and love. It's a wonder it doesn't blow the avenue apart." While the brothers have managed to reconnect, the complexity of life remains.

And here again, a writer might locate an ending. A reader might be well satisfied, sufficiently rewarded for having taken the time and expended the effort to read. Yet readers, like audiences of all kinds, love an encore, and a great encore can be essential to a performance, as is the case in "Sonny's Blues."

An invitation has been extended and accepted to go to a Village nightclub to hear Sonny play. And so eagerly we go.

The entirety of Act III occurs in two scenes. The first scene covers approximately six and a quarter pages, beginning with the older brother at the window and ending with the two brothers reunited. Across the six pages, the scene is composed of short, complete movements of conflict, action, and resolution, as is the first act scene between the older brother and the raggy boy, and as is the dramatic structure in scenes throughout the story. The second scene in Act III, from the brothers entering the night club to the end of the story, covers about four and a half pages, making the act ten and three quarter pages long. Act I runs nine and a quarter pages. Act II runs twelve pages. In other words, from act to act, the structure is roughly proportional, with the first act being slightly shorter than the other two; the second act slightly longer. This sort of symmetry in a three-act structure occurs fairly often in masterly story writing, though with variations according to the nature of the story being told. Often the beginning of a story will occur in short movements to bring a reader in quickly and easily. Then, through the middle of the story, as the characters and conflicts gather complexity and weight, the movements will lengthen, after which the pace may quicken and the movements shorten, signaling an approach to the end. Such structures orient readers temporally in a story. Baldwin, or any accomplished author, does not use this three-part structure formulaically but recognizes it in harmony with the span of life—youth, maturity, old age—and with sexual rhythms, which are akin to narrative rhythms.

Between the first and second scenes of Act III, a line space occurs, indicating a shift in time and place, from the older brother's apartment to the Village nightclub on a short, dark downtown street. The brothers make their way through a noisy, tightly packed crowd toward a big, dimly lit room where the bandstand is. A voice erupts out of the darkness, saying, "Hello, boy," and an enormous, older Black man puts his arm around Sonny. The man has a voice as big as he is, and he says he's been sitting right there waiting for Sonny. Sonny grins, pulls a little away, and introduces his brother and the big man. Sonny casually mentions that he's told the man about his brother—a small but telling gesture about Sonny's care and love as distinct from the fear that long ruled the brother. The big man's name is Creole.

Consider that Baldwin might have chosen any name at all for the character. Why Creole?

Because Creole embodies multiple races—European, African, Caribbean, Native American. Names are images. Creole is an image of unity. All tribes in one.

Creole shakes the older brother's hand and says he's glad to meet him, calling him *son*. Baldwin puts the words *boy* and *son* into Creole's mouth—words that when addressed to or about a Black man might convey condescension or worse, but from Creole they ring with good humor and affection, even merriment. Baldwin purposefully shifts commonly used racially toned slurs into playfully warm familiarities. In the world of "Sonny's Blues," where fathers are missing, broken, compromised, or fearful, Creole emerges from the dark as a good father, if not a holy man or god in a house of music. With light touches, the story turns a potentially derogatory use of *boy* into a glad welcome and the diminutive *sonny* back into its root *son*, granting the brothers majority and conferring father-to-son lineage.

The older brother narrates that it was clear Creole was glad to meet him for Sonny's sake. Smiling, Creole tells the brother,

"You got a real musician in *your* family." With these enthusiastic words, Creole has brought something forward that the older brother has been missing all along. The reader may have missed it, too, from the beginning of the story with the news of Sonny's arrest—that is, people get busted all the time for heroin and are not written up about it in the newspaper. The reason Sonny's arrest made the news was that he'd already been making his mark as a musician. As a jazz pianist, Sonny is the real deal. The older brother just hasn't been able to credit or understand it. Creole takes his arm from around Sonny and slaps him affectionately with the back of his hand—a jocular form of love and respect, acknowledging the importance of the occasion for Sonny, who's only two weeks out of jail, and Creole wants to help Sonny by keeping things light in the moments before he goes onstage.

One of Sonny's bandmates comes up and loudly begins teasing him, telling the older brother all sorts of terrible things about Sonny. Again, like Creole, the bandmate is cheerfully imparting affection and keeping things loose. They understand the performance anxiety that Sonny would naturally have after so much time away.

Almost everyone at the bar knows Sonny. Some of them are musicians, some are hangers-on. The older brother is introduced to everyone, and they're all very polite to him. His awareness of Sonny's stature grows by the moment; he's in Sonny's world, his kingdom, and there's no question that Sonny's veins bear royal blood.

Creole gives the older brother a dark corner table, and he watches the band horsing around in front of the bandstand, laughing and gesturing at each other, staying just outside the spotlight on the stage, as if by stepping into that light too quickly, they might go up in flames. Timing is everything, and Baldwin takes time and care to prepare for and build up to the performance so that it will have its maximum effect. The drummer, who was the one loudly teasing Sonny, takes his place at his kit. Then Creole, humorously, ceremoniously leads Sonny by the arm to the piano. A woman calls out to Sonny, and others applaud. Sonny, being funny and ceremonious in his own way and touched almost to the point of tears, doesn't hide or show his emotion but rides it "like a man," grinning and putting his hands to his heart and bowing. All these simple gestures, along with Baldwin's careful staging and pacing of the scene, produce a deeply felt, extremely moving sense of Sonny's vulnerability, a belief in him, and a desire to see him play and succeed. These elements touch any reader's sense of personal frailties and strengths—the desire for self-expression, growth, and fulfillment. At this point, when reading "Sonny's Blues" aloud to students, I can with difficulty usually keep my throat from thickening and causing me to break off reading, while students' faces fill with the emotional struggle Baldwin so tenderly plays. The musicality that gathers throughout the story, and now the lyric movement underlying and supporting the approach to the bandstand scene, comes fully forward as a jazz quartet performance. The poet Stanley Kunitz, writing about prosody, made the following observations:

> [Rhythm can be experienced] as a complex of thoughts and feelings looking for a language, seeking a language.

> Even before it is ready to change into language, a poem may begin to assert its buried life in the mind with wordless surges of rhythm and counter-rhythm. Gradually the rhythms attach themselves to objects and feelings.[4]

The jazz performance and overall lyricism in "Sonny's Blues" rest on the principles noted by Kunitz. Drawing on his observations, I would describe the lyric movement that runs through "Sonny's Blues" as thoughts and emotions riding the back of actions to a point of illumination. Baldwin, having brought Sonny to the bandstand, will bring everything in the story together as revelation.

In our era, with the proliferation of so many forms of media and so much information and entertainment streaming 24/7 on myriad devices, an overwhelming atmosphere has arisen, in which all opinions may seem to be equal and valid. When all things seem to matter equally, nothing may seem to matter enough, which is a loss. Alternatively, crowd popularity can tend to stand in as the guarantor of assessed quality for a work or performance. Then another kind of loss can occur. Mostly unexamined acceptance of received opinions and general acclaim supplant the appropriate sense of awe—reverential respect—that should attend encounters with works or performances that are truly awesome. A kind of numbness can set in. Accumulation of data points replaces felt experience. Quantification supersedes qualification. When sharing stories with other readers and writers, I listen for the moments when awe takes hold. Then, silence. No one speaks.

Creole takes up his bass fiddle, a lean brown man picks up his horn, the band is ready, and the atmosphere in the room tightens.

[4] Stanley Kunitz, "Action and Incantation," in *The Structure of Verse*, ed. Harvey Gross (New York: Ecco), 256, 258.

The crowd begins to quiet, the waitress runs around taking last orders, lovers snuggle a little closer to each other, and the stage lights turn *indigo*. As with *copper* and *Creole*, Baldwin's choice of the word *indigo* adds dimension to the story. The word lends a realistic nightclub aura and depth of mood. The color is often associated with intuition, integrity, and fairness, and its purple hue attaches to royalty. But indigo also summons the history of slavery. In the mid-eighteenth century the importation of slaves into North America ramped up as a result of a booming European demand for indigo as a basis of blue dye. Indigo soon became the main export in South Carolina, leading Georgia to end its ban on slavery in 1751. Fifteen years later, the enslaved population of Georgia numbered 18,000. Then, with the end of the Revolutionary War, Britain turned to forced sharecropper labor in India to supply indigo, while in America rice and cotton supplanted indigo as the slavery-dependent cash crops, but worldwide indigo had already created a legacy of slavery. Remembrance of that legacy casts a light on the musicians in "Sonny's Blues." Creole looks around him, making sure the band is with him, and then with a jump he strikes his fiddle, and they play.

Baldwin writes (the older brother narrates):

> All I know about music is that not many people ever really hear it. And even then, on the rare occasions when something opens within, and the music enters, what we mainly hear, or hear corroborated, are personal, private, vanishing evocations. But the man who creates the music is hearing something else, is dealing with the roar rising from the void and imposing order on it as it hits the air. What is evoked in him, then, is of another order, more terrible because it has no words, and triumphant, too, for that same reason. And his triumph, when he triumphs, is ours.

With music as the metaphor, the passage begins by addressing the common circumstance of white noise, cliché, subjectivity, and relative inattention that daily and necessarily cloud ordinary human communication—necessarily, because being fully and accurately articulate, much less original and strikingly expressive, as well as being keenly, constantly receptive in every moment would frustrate and exhaust most efforts, so humanity accepts and depends on approximated intercourse. Because each individual is the main character of his or her own story, each tends to attune to what momentarily touches his or her immediate self. Moments pass, things change, much is forgotten, misremembered, or lost, yet the self focuses, as it often must, on its own immediacy. The passage then draws a distinction between common experience and the truly creative act of an artist. Baldwin calls on the same formal principles of lyricism as Kunitz observed and, marvelously, anyone reading "Sonny's Blues," truly reading it, experiences Baldwin dealing with the roar from the void and imposing order on it and partakes with him in celebratory triumph over chaos and darkness.

Meanwhile, Sonny struggles at the piano. He's troubled, working hard, and not with it. His brother has the feeling that his bandmates are waiting for him and prodding him along. But then, watching Creole, the brother understands that Creole is holding them back. He has them on a tight rein. He's keeping the beat, wailing on the bass, eyes half closed, listening, having a dialogue with Sonny. He wants Sonny to strike out for the depths without fear of drowning. Creole listens to hear Sonny do the things on the keys that will say he's all the way in.

And while Creole listens, Sonny moves in torment. Baldwin writes (the older brother narrates):

> I had never thought before of how awful the relationship must be between the musician and his instrument. He has to fill it, the instrument, with the breath of life, his own. He has to make it do what he wants it to do. And a piano is just a piano. It's made of so much wood and wires and little hammers and big ones, and ivory. While there's only so much you can do with it, the only way to find out is to try; to try and make it do everything.

The passage pertains not only to music but to all art and human creativity. Only God creates out of nothing; the rest of us work with what we've been given. A valuable test for an artist to take regarding the quality of his or her work is to consider, Is there more here than what I started with? If there's not, or only as much as was given, or less, then the work has not yet been done. The *more* can come only from the artist's own soul. More connectedness, more meaning, more possibility, and enhancement of life. The gift the artist gives. Another way to think about this is that God, or Nature, gives life, and after giving life, God is essentially indifferent, leaving us on our own to determine what we'll do with what we've been given. The gift, like Nature itself, is good and bad at the same time, and seldom are those aspects evenly given. In Baldwin's Harlem, as in all Black America, the burden of suffering greatly outweighs any sense of a benign God. Reality runs counter to the idea that God is only good. But in "Sonny's Blues" Baldwin carefully balances faith and unbelief. The cloth of the story is woven from biblical allusion, cadence, church music and imagery, and the mother's faith, within all of which Sonny's prison letter briefly denies faith and, later, the older brother momentarily sees that not a soul has been rescued or believes in the holiness of revivalists. Baldwin poses all this in such a way that the reader can decide according to his or her own beliefs about salvation. Baldwin doesn't insist, but his view is humanist. His concern is with the here and now. He seeks to encourage everyone's participation and kinship in improving the quality of all lives on Earth. And given the circumstances of his life—not only his race but also his challenges as an illegitimate son and as a gay man living through a time and attitudes adverse to his nature—his clarity and generosity of spirit are breathtaking. I once heard him give a reading at the 92nd Street Y in Manhattan. The house was full, an audience of 1,500 or so, mostly thirty-something urban Black professionals. After the reading, there was a Q & A period, and a well-dressed young Black man seated in the middle of the auditorium raised his hand and asked, "Mr. Baldwin, can you tell us why you left the country and went to Paris instead of staying here and fighting the fight." It was more of a statement than a question, and I can only imagine either that the man wasn't familiar with Baldwin's life work and his commitment to social justice—with his being, for instance, among the first marchers across the Pettus Bridge in Selma in 1963 and giving himself to many other occasions for the cause of civil rights—or that he rather unthinkingly needed to assert himself and his generation at the forefront of change. Baldwin was not a physically large man. He was diminutive. He came out from behind the lectern, and he was furious. He walked to the lip of the stage, and it was as if his body, in spite of being diminutive, arched out, bending over the audience so he could lean right down into his questioner's face. With barely restrained ferocity, Baldwin said, "If I could have gotten a job as anything other than a dishwasher, I would have stayed." The audience held its breath, and then Baldwin went back to the lectern and took other questions as if nothing had happened. Baldwin was often asked about leaving the US for Paris, and he could be touchy about it. His life's journey understandably entailed the question of identity, *Who am I?*—not a simple question for an illegitimately born, Black, gay, highly intelligent, talented, sensitive man who became renowned. Like any famous person, he had to try to maintain his integrity amid the disorienting effects of any and all projections directed toward him. Sonny's trial at the piano can be seen, in part, as corresponding to Baldwin's evolution as a writer. Baldwin's work gives an impression of easy mastery, but it could not have been easy to be him and to translate his experience and knowing into art.

In an essay "The Uses of the Blues," Baldwin writes:

> I'm talking about what happens to you if, having barely escaped suicide, or death, or madness, or yourself, you watch your children growing up and no matter what you do, no matter what you do, you are powerless, you are really powerless, against the force of the world that is out to tell your child that he has no right to be alive. And no amount of liberal jargon, and no amount of talk about how well and how far we have progressed, does anything to soften or to point out any solution to this dilemma. In every generation, ever since Negroes have been here, every Negro mother and father has had to face that child and try to create in that child some way of surviving this particular world, some way to make the child who will be despised not despise himself.[5]

In the course of his lifetime, Baldwin survived several suicide attempts. Sonny's struggles to transcend his circumstances and to create art convey an attempt to make every life more human

[5] James Baldwin, "The Uses of the Blues," *The Cross of Redemption* (New York: Pantheon, 2010), 83.

in terms of joy, freedom, and the respect that people can have for one another.

Sonny hasn't been near a piano or out in the world in over a year. His sobriety and his relationship with himself and his brother are newly formed. He plays haltingly, starting in one direction and then going in another, panicked, marking time, starting over, getting stuck. Sonny's moment at the keyboard is the culmination of a series of conversations that form the structure of the story:

- the older brother's conversation with himself at the beginning of the story;
- his unwilling conversation with Sonny's friend, the raggy boy;
- the rapprochement letters between the brothers while Sonny is in jail;
- the brothers' tentative talk when Sonny is released from jail, including the backstory of talk with teenage Sonny dreaming of India and escape from Harlem;
- the older brother's last conversation with his mother and her behest that he always be there for Sonny;
- after the mother's death, the fraught conversation between the brothers concerning music and Sonny moving in with Isabel and her parents;
- Sonny's break with Isabel and her parents over his skipping school;
- the angry break between the brothers after Sonny returns from the army;
- and, finally, the first scene of Act III, in which Sonny makes his confession, breaks through his brother's denial, and finds acceptance.

The psychology and interplay throughout these conversations that lead to breakthrough provide the basis for the story's final scene, in which Sonny tries to find his way again through every mistake, resistance, fear, and possible path in order to improvise a musical breakthrough. But whereas the earlier scenes depend on the relative success or failure of connection between two characters, the final scene depends on Sonny's being able, or not, to carry the hard-won truth telling and wholeness he achieved with his brother into an expressive connection with the music, his bandmates, and the audience (which includes the reader)—that is to say, the personal or individual drama plays out toward the collective.

Watching his face, the brother sees Sonny as never before. Everything that was once apparent about Sonny burns away, while hidden parts of him burn in with the fury of his battle.

Near the end of the first set Creole's face seems to show that something's changed in the music, something the brother didn't hear. The band finishes to scattered applause, and without warning Creole begins almost sardonically playing "Am I Blue?" But why sardonically?

Creole and the band are playing an instrumental version, but the lyrics of the blues standard are well known. Here's Billie Holiday's version:

Am I blue, am I blue
Ain't these tears in my eyes telling you
Am I blue, you'd be too
If each plan with your man done fell through

Was a time I was his only one
But now I'm the sad and lonely one, lonely
Was I gay till today
Now he's gone and we're through, am I blue

Was I gay till today
Now he's gone and we're through, am I blue
Oh he's gone, he left me, am I blue[6]

Her 1941 performance with the Eddie Heywood Orchestra gives a lush, and touch romantic, upbeat lift to the song's undertow of abandonment, sorrow, and loneliness. An earlier version, Ethel Waters's 1929 release, has a somewhat more sentimental serio-comic tone. Waters appeared in a film version surrounded by a troupe of smiling cotton pickers with cutaway shots of a white society couple in top hat and gown looking gaily down on the scene made for their entertainment. Baldwin's tonal suggestion via Creole picks up on Sonny's slap at Louis Armstrong and his consigning "Tis' the Old Ship of Zion" to terribleness. Creole's mockery of "Am I Blue?" seems to say, *Enough. Listen to what we can do instead with what we've been given.*

Taking Creole's hint, Sonny really begins to play. Creole and the band let loose, creating a sound at first "dry, and driving, beautiful and calm and old." At last Sonny's with it, as if he has a brand-new piano and can't get over it.

Then Creole strikes something deep and tight, bringing apprehension into the air, reminding the audience what the blues are about but also making the music new. Baldwin's words bring the feeling of the music alive, but to hear what the shift from old to new sounds like, I suggest listening to Holiday's "Am I Blue?" and then following it with Coltrane's "A Love Supreme." The older brother's description of the performance in "Sonny's Blues" could well be of the Coltrane piece:

[6] "Am I Blue?" (from *On with the Show*), lyrics by Grant Clarke and music by Harry Akst. © 1929 (renewed), WC Music Corp. All Rights Reserved. Used by Permission of Alfred Music.

> [Creole and his boys] were keeping it new, at the risk of ruin, destruction, madness, and death, in order to find new ways to make us listen. For, while the tale of how we suffer, and how we are delighted, and we may triumph is never new, it always must be heard. There isn't any other tale to tell, it's the only light we've got in all this darkness.

On the bass, Creole seems to be saying, *Listen. Listen to Sonny.* Creole and the band wish him Godspeed, and Sonny solos, the band coming in with touches saying *amen.*

Sonny takes the music all the way back to the beginning of "Am I Blue?" but makes it his own, slowly, and no longer a lament. He suggests that lamenting can cease and freedom will arrive if everyone listens. The battle shows in his face, and in the music his brother hears all that Sonny's been through and will continue to go through. His hands on the keys suggest the long line of generations and remembrance, death and rebirth, and the older brother thinks of his mother and what she suffered and of the death of his father's brother and the loss of his own little girl and of his wife's tears. His own tears begin to rise, and yet he's "aware that this was only a moment, that the world waited outside, as hungry as a tiger, and that trouble stretched above us, longer than the sky."

Then it's over. Creole and Sonny let out a breath. They're soaking and grinning. And Baldwin nails his virtuoso rendition of the performance with the older brother observing, "There was a lot of applause and some of it was real." So true, always. The quick observation harkens back to the earlier comment that not many people ever really hear the music that they're listening to. And it can also be said that not many people actually see what they're looking at. Baldwin encourages acuity, attention to what's true.

A compelling story in the vein of realism usually depends on there being at least two well-matched, equally weighted characters who together embody the conflict, or paradox, to be worked out in the main plot of the story. Along with the two primary characters, an author ordinarily develops several other characters, each of whose story forms a complete subplot that interacts with the main plot and the other subplots to create a more fully dimensional drama and convincing reality than could otherwise be created. In "Sonny's Blues," Sonny and the older brother carry the main plot, while the obvious subplots flow from the older brother's students, the raggy boy, the barmaid, the mother, the roomful of old folks and kids at evening, the father and his brother, Isabel and her parents, Grace, and Creole and the band. Each of the subplots has its relative duration—some brief, some longer—and each has a beginning, middle, and end (with a conflict, action, and resolution structure), comprising a rounded, conclusive drama of its own while adding substance and significance to the story as a whole. Baldwin accords each character his or her own reality and desire, and during each character's time onstage, the character has parity with the other characters. Baldwin doesn't use his characters as functions of his intentions but grants them their individual lives. He doesn't condescend to his characters and thus doesn't condescend to the reader. Each character and subplot, if viewed as apart from the main line of the story, can be appreciated as a smaller drama of its own, and because each subplot has its integrity and forms an essential element of the main plot, the story achieves a unity that would be at best partial if the subplots were only interdependent.

At the end of the set, the older brother asks the waitress to take drinks to the bandstand. There's a pause while the bandmates talk among themselves, standing in the indigo light. After a while the waitress puts a Scotch and milk on top of the piano for Sonny. He doesn't seem to notice it, but just as the band starts playing again, he takes a sip and nods to his brother. For him, then, the tumbler of Scotch and milk glows and shakes above Sonny's head "like the very cup of trembling." These final words of the story resonate all the way back through to the beginning, drawing everything together.

Such a powerful ending, so simply done and saying so much. Baldwin testifies that the triumph of love over fear is never final but must be fought and won again and again, day by day, moment to moment, and that dire necessity, which anyone might well wish to deny, calls on everyone to engage on behalf of love.

The glass of Scotch and milk brings together all the dark and light imagery in the story. It also suggests that what was empty is full again. The mixture is a drink preferred by someone with a sensitive stomach or ulcers and evokes Sonny's turmoil and vulnerability and universal human frailty.

Cup of trembling alludes to biblical prophecy and betokens God's promise to punish wrongdoing and to bring his wrath down on those who persecute his people.[7] At the end of "Sonny's Blues" the cup represents both the commonality of all peoples and a stark warning that without racial harmony ruin will inevitably come.

[7] Isaiah 51:9, 17, 22 and Zechariah 12:2.

EPILOGUE

One Sunday in 2021, when I was first beginning to think about writing this book, my wife Carol Edgarian and I took a Christmas walk along the San Francisco Bay with Tobias and Catherine Wolff. I'd been rereading "Sonny's Blues" and was enthusing about it to Toby, and he related an anecdote concerning Baldwin. Toby's older brother Geoffrey had met Baldwin in Istanbul, and later when both men were living in New York City, Geoffrey invited Baldwin for dinner. He also invited some others, including Toby, who was a young man aspiring and destined to follow his older brother in becoming a noted author, and like the other guests, Toby was very excited at the prospect of meeting Baldwin. At the appointed hour, everyone had arrived except Baldwin. The wait for him lengthened. Wine was drunk, dinner not served. Hours passed. The guests drooped, and finally, downcast and perplexed at what had happened, Geoffrey and his guests gave up. It was clear that Baldwin wouldn't arrive. Eventually, Geoffrey discovered that his building's white doorman would not let Baldwin enter and would not call up to Geoffrey's apartment to announce his guest.

Stories end but take new form in other stories. Edward P. Jones's short story "All Aunt Hagar's Children" takes its title from the biblical story of Hagar in Genesis. Abraham's wife Sarah, who was seemingly sterile and could not bear children, told Abraham she would give him her Egyptian slave Hagar as a wife to bear a child. Hagar conceived and bore a son, Ishmael, and Sarah in turn began to despise Hagar. In time, Sarah conceived and bore a son, Isaac, and she commanded Abraham to cast out Hagar, which he did, but God sent an angel to Hagar with his promise that the boy would be the progenitor of a great nation. Various interpretations have descended from this tale, usually concerning the division of tribes—Jews and Arabs, Jews and Christians, men and women, or, as in the Jones story, Blacks and whites. Jones's rendition of the tale is a retrospective first-person narration on the part of a young Black man recently returned from service in the Korean War and planning to leave his childhood home in Washington, DC, soon to search for gold in Alaska, where he believes a man can be a real man. But he's not destined to go. His mother, her sister Penny, and their childhood friend Miss Agatha call on him with a request that amounts to a command to find out who murdered Agatha's son Ike, a crime that's gone unsolved for two years and that the police have shown no interest in pursuing. The story takes places during approximately the same era as "Sonny's Blues," the late 1950s, and a brief structural comparison reveals similarities. Both stories occur in three acts. The front story in "Sonny's Blues" runs from the time the older brother reads about Sonny's arrest up to the end of the evening in the Village nightclub, or a little more than one year, with particular focus on the two weeks from when Sonny gets out of jail until he plays with the band in the nightclub. The backstory in "Sonny's Blues" reaches to the early 1900s when the father's brother was run over in the road and killed by drunken white men. In "Aunt Hagar" the front story takes places across two and half weeks of the hero's clueless search for the killer, with a backstory that touches the antebellum world of slavery and, as in "Sonny's Blues," contains an inheritance of violence, murder, and consequent hard sacrifices made in the effort to keep family members safe. Each story accurately conveys the tone, atmosphere, and physical layout of its respective city so that even if a reader has never been to New York City or Washington, DC, an intimate acquaintance with the setting occurs in the reading, and the real-life streets and neighborhoods form a structural element of the fiction.

The perspective of the first-person narration in both stories brings knowing from beyond the end of the story, though not too far removed from the time of the stories' events, thus indicating a sense of racial conditions that pertain right on up to today. And whereas Baldwin's narrator exhibits his struggle with denial, along with his concern and need for his brother, Jones's narrator shows cautious resentment over being denied his own way in the world, while being inwardly tender and caring—similar adaptive tensions in men whose existence is threatened by the fact of their race. Both narrators dwell on cruel circumstances yet handle them with touches of humor, buoying and carrying the reader on better aspirations. In both stories, the mother is a central moral force, though the mother in "Aunt Hagar," having necessarily committed violence as a girl, protecting her friend Agatha from rape by a white man, presents as a somewhat tougher and more stringent woman than the mother in "Sonny's Blues." Biblical allusion, religious imagery, and the sense of heaven and hell as being of the here and now run though both stories. They share a confluence of darkness and light and show the effects of heroin and alcohol taken to dull the pain of suffering, but whereas Baldwin concludes by mixing hope for racial reconciliation with dire prophetic warning, Jones indicates that circumstances have in some ways worsened since Baldwin's time, but in the end, using similar imagery to Baldwin's, Jones draws a potentially more optimistic picture.

Jones's nameless protagonist works as an clerk for a Jewish lawyer, who lives above the office with his wife Dvera (a name that connotes *truth*, an element of meaning she provides to the story). The lawyer is a mensch, caring and generous, but the employer-employee situation evokes the familiar inner-city tension between Black tenants and Jewish landlords and shopkeepers, another example of tribal divisions, and the protagonist has been so schooled in the danger of a Black man being uppity or seeming to be untoward with a white woman that he avoids Dvera and regards her with distaste. Meanwhile, as he meanders on his murder investigation, he's haunted by the dying words of a white woman who fell right in front of him in the street. He tried to resuscitate her and, as she died, held her hand, all the while fearing what people would think. The woman's last words are unintelligible, "A moll is gav vain ah rav und ah rabbit sin," and "Zetcha kender lock, gadank za tira vos ear lair rent doe," and they repeat in his mind over and over. The phrases have a deep lyric pull, and he recites them aloud to himself, wishing he could have saved the woman, in spite of his general disaffection toward women other than as casual sex partners. As in "Sonny's Blues," in "Hagar" grown men and fathers are scarce. The protagonist labors under what he experiences as his mother's preference for girls and women and her constant reproaches of him. Then one day Dvera overhears the protagonist reciting the dead woman's words and weeps, alarming him that he'll be blamed for upsetting her. He can't look at her. He gazes at the floor. But she calms and explains that the words were ones her father used when telling her stories to comfort her when the world got to be too much. So, now, added to the history and consequences of slavery as part of the story, there's the specter of the Holocaust and pogroms carried out against the Jews. Metaphorically, the story opens out to embody all persecutions of tribes at the hands of other tribes, the chief protection against which lies in the love and care of family and in human understanding and kindness, especially in the absence of social justice.

Unable to solve the murder and fed up with trying and with the women having asked him to solve it in the first place, the protagonist decides to tell Agatha that her son Ike was killed by a man who has since died. He rationalizes that it doesn't matter if he wrongly blames a dead man, though he knows his mother would have something to say about that. As his conscience turns in him, he accidently stumbles on the truth—the killer was Ike's wife, whom Ike had badly mistreated and betrayed, and it seems apparent that Aggie has known all along that the killer was her beloved daughter-in-law, who is also the mother of a little granddaughter named after Agatha. (Ike, like Sonny, was a heroin addict but a mean one and without redeeming qualities past his boyhood. His mother knew what he was like, but still he was her son.)

The protagonist takes this news to his mother, who tells him, "You decide what you must tell Aggie and then leave her in peace after that... She knows what she knows. Maybe she needed someone like you in the world to know it too. The only harm we ever done you was for you own good and you must not forget that." These words, though they may not sound like it, are the mother's benediction. When she and the two other women commissioned the protagonist to solve the crime, they were instinctively saying to him, *Time for you to grow up, face the truth of the world, and take your place in it. We've done all we could for you, and now you must live your life.* The protagonist begins to understand that he would not find gold in Alaska if his life depended on it—it was a boyish dream—and he will not be leaving DC. As this scene plays out the mother sits at her kitchen table, holding a cup with both hands, and in the cup are two-thirds milk and one-third coffee, dark and light, the cup of trembling quietly evoked.

The protagonist returns to the lawyer's office and finds that Dvera has translated the dying woman's words from the correct Yiddish, which he misheard, into English: "Once upon a time there was a rabbi and his wife . . . Listen, children, remember, precious ones, what you're learning here." And that's exactly what Jones is saying to the reader and demonstrating as the power of storytelling.

The protagonist goes upstairs from the office into the lawyer's apartment, where he has never dared venture before, and all his apprehension around Dvera has fallen away. She's on the phone with her husband, who is in Israel, and their conversation is that of a happy conjugal pair—in effect, a rabbi and his wife, an image that offers a restored balance between the masculine and feminine in the world of the story. The protagonist's tone of caution and resentment falls away, and his vision of the world around him brightens. He looks out a window, which, as in the Baldwin story, is a recurrent image of altered perception, and he sees "six little colored girls" and his eyes settle

> on a girl in a yellow dress . . . the sun was full upon her face. Her long plaits swung with her in an almost miraculous way. It was good to

> watch her, because I had never seen anything like that in Washington in my whole life. I followed her until she disappeared. It would have been nice to know what was on her mind.[1]

The image of six little girls doubles the protagonist's mother, Aunt Penny, and Miss Agatha, who as young girls survived a white man's attack. The doubling is an amplification confirming the miraculousness of life. The radiance, joy, and wonder evoked at the end speak to the future—the next generation and the potentially affirmative possibilities that await it.

On the way to this uplifting outcome, however, the story posits that Ike "was one of only sixty-six people murdered in DC" the first year that the protagonist was away while serving in Korea. That would have been in the mid- to late 1950s. Writing that statistic into the story, Jones, a native of DC, would have been well aware that since the 1950s the murder rate in DC and other American cities has only gone up, nearly quadrupling in DC across the past couple of decades, while the DC population from the 1950s to today has decreased by approximately 25 percent. Moreover, in 1957 DC became the first majority Black major city in the US. So who's killing whom? Set in 1950s Harlem, "Sonny's Blues" indicates that whites are killing Blacks and that Blacks are at continuing risk of killing themselves with drugs and other self-abuses. "Aunt Hagar," set in 1950s DC but written five decades later than "Sonny's Blues," indicates the same deathly circumstances as in "Sonny Blues," with an added awareness of the worsened reality that today, in cities large and small, racial and socioeconomic circumstances have deteriorated and become

[1] Edward P. Jones, "All Aunt Hagar's Children," *The New Yorker*, December 22 and 29, 2003, 129.

so constrained that Blacks have been killing Blacks, but I think what Jones means for the reader to understand is essentially that *we are killing each other and ourselves.* And *we* includes everyone. No one of any race can be free of the effects of generations of racial oppression so long as it continues.

An interviewer once asked Jones what he would tell an aspiring writer to read for inspiration, and Jones replied:

> What I would do, I would start with the Bible. Not for any religious reason, but for all the stories. I mean, you have Lot. And an angel comes to the door. He doesn't know it's an angel, but it's a visitor and you're supposed to treat visitors like royalty. Well, the townsmen in the story come up, and they tell Lot to send out the visitor so that they can molest him. Well, the visitor is royalty, so Lot gives them his daughter. You can come up with something comparable in the twenty-first century. Hell, that's one of the reasons why I watched those court things, when I had a TV. Judge Judy had a case where a woman took her ex-husband to court because she wanted money to pay for the burial of their son. And it comes out, in court, that the father possibly knew who killed his son, but because he didn't want to be a snitch, he didn't say. Now, you can see the mother's side of it, of course. But what is it in a man that he could say, I love my son, but there's a code. I can't break the code. That's the stuff literature is made of. Stupid codes where love means nothing.[2]

This central concern with the action of love is evident in "Aunt Hagar," as it is in "Sonny's Blues." Though both stories are grounded in faith and religious motifs, neither story is religious in an ordinary churchy sense but rather in the root meaning of *religion*, or the Latin *relegere*—to go through, or read again. In other

[2] Edward P. Jones, "The Art of Fiction," *The Paris Review* 222, no. 207 (winter 2013), https://www.theparisreview.org/interviews/6283/the-art-of-fiction-no-222-edward-p-jones.

words, the action of religion is to link back to what's come before and to carry life meaningfully forward into the future. As Eudora Welty put it in her novel *The Optimist's Daughter*, "For her life, any life, she had to believe, was nothing but the continuity of its love."[3] Baldwin and Jones share that belief and exhibit it in their stories. In retelling the biblical tale of Hagar and Ishmael's expulsion, Jones performs a profound, monumental creative act, transforming an ancient myth, renewing it, with the message that we do not have to be apart after all; the tribes can be together. What was sundered in Genesis and grew to define the alienation of peoples from each other, Jones brings back together thousands of years later. *Listen, children, remember, precious ones, what you're learning here,* he so tenderly says, and Baldwin at the end of "Sonny's Blues" makes the same entreaty: "I understood at last that [Sonny] could help us to be free if we would listen, that he would never be free until we did."

In both stories, listening engenders seeing, or witnessing. Sonny's brother sees the long line that connects generations, understands the fragility of life and, in likening the tumbler of Scotch and milk to *the very cup of trembling,* gives a stronger, more explicit expression of the opposed paths of redemption and destruction than does Jones's protagonist, whose conclusion lifts completely away from senselessness and darkness, returning the reader to the world outside the story with a sense of wonder. Jones doesn't have to end by emphasizing crisis in the same way that Baldwin has already done. Instead, with the mother's cup of coffee and milk, Jones alludes quietly, almost invisibly to Baldwin, who was writing a half dozen years ahead of the 1964

[3] Eudora Welty, *The Optimist's Daughter* (New York: Vintage, 1969), 160.

Civil Rights Act. Jones comes thirty years later, and in "Aunt Hager" having reached all the way back into Genesis, and into antebellum Alabama slavery, and having shown the things that have not improved but only gotten worse since the end of slavery, and having implicitly indicated all that has not yet been solved by law, he offers an image of an unspoiled or redeemed future. He's earned the right to offer it by the thoroughness, rigor, and artfulness of his storytelling, by the fact of his accomplishments, and moreover by his very existence. Whenever I read "All Aunt Hagar's Children" and get to the concluding image of the little Black girl twirling in a yellow dress, the sun full upon her face, I'm reminded of Langston Hughes's poem "Dream Variation":

To fling my arms wide
In some place of the sun,
To whirl and to dance
Till the white day is done.
Then rest at cool evening
Beneath a tall tree
While night comes on gently,
Dark like me—
That is my dream!

To fling my arms wide
In the face of the sun,
Dance! Whirl! Whirl!
Till the quick day is done.
Rest at pale evening . . .
A tall, slim tree . . .
Night coming tenderly
Black like me.[4]

[4] Langston Hughes, "Dream Variation," *The Weary Blues* (1926; repr., New York: Dover, 2022), 21. Page numbers refer to the Dover edition.

Four decades before Martin Luther King's "I Have a Dream" speech raised a call for racial equality, unity, justice, and freedom, twenty-four-year-old Langston Hughes published his first book, a poetry collection, *The Weary Blues* (1926). The title poem features a street corner blues singer on Lenox Avenue, one of the *vivid, killing streets* of "Sonny Blues." The blues player sings:

I got the Weary Blues
And I can't be satisfied.
  Got the Weary Blues
And can't be satisfied—
I ain't happy no mo'
And I wish that I had died.[5]

It's a classic blues lament of an oppressed soul. In contrast, "Dream Variation," from the same collection, is a song of a soul that's self-loving, whole, and free. It comes amid the Harlem Renaissance, an early-twentieth-century period of Black creativity and hope that spread internationally and continues to inspire but whose suggestion of human progress had not been fulfilled by the time Baldwin wrote "Sonny's Blues" and has not been completed today. *The Fire Next Time,* which preceded King's "Dream" speech (August 1963) by ten months, comes out of Baldwin's recognition that the American public wasn't listening enough and did not sufficiently appreciate the consequences of inattention and inaction. A more urgent message needed to be delivered, and Baldwin had already achieved more than enough recognition to carry his testimony out to the world. The title of the book-length essay alludes to apocalyptic destruction. He exhorts:

[5] Hughes, "Dream Variation," 3.

> If we do not now dare everything, the fulfillment of that prophecy, recreated from the Bible in song by a slave, is upon us: God gave Noah the rainbow sign, No more water, the fire next time![6]

As telling as *the cup of trembling* in "Sonny's Blues" would be for anyone well familiar with Old Testament scripture but not necessarily clear in its complete import for anyone unacquainted with Bible verses, Baldwin made his argument in *The Fire Next Time* unmistakable, and his prophetic warning of destruction came true in rioting in cities across the US, following the assassination of Martin Luther King. In the fifty-some years since, incidents of civil unrest in the face of racial oppression have at times receded but have not gone away, and will not go away so long as injustice prevails.

In 2008 Barack Obama's election as forty-fourth president of the United States seemed to herald America's arrival at the promised land. Robert Kennedy in the 1960s several times expressed his assurance that within thirty to forty years "a Negro" could be elected president of the United States.[7] Listening to Kennedy making this statement to the world via Voice of America radio and reading his words to the same effect in the text of speeches given during a period of turbulent racial strife, one recognizes a degree of political spin or propaganda, or at least characteristic Kennedy idealism in putting the best view forward, but his politics and idealism do not much undercut the man's will and desire to see justice prevail. And his prediction came true. Obama's election was an exhilarating cause for hope and celebration, especially for children of color with their lifetimes ahead of them. But instead of progressed societal harmony, Obama's

[6] Baldwin, *Fire Next Time*, 141.

[7] Robert Kennedy, "Robert Kennedy's 1961 Prediction," Voice of America, May 23, 1961, YouTube video, https://www.youtube.com/watch?v=oD7a8k5kyGw.

presence in the White House, newly remarked for having been built by slave labor, aroused the fears and biases of many who have felt marginalized or threatened with becoming so. Aggression and violence have escalated.

One might hope that the rise of white supremacist organizations and related phenomena are a last gasp of evils in an existential struggle. One can hope that the increasingly diverse makeup of the American population will break racism's hold on society. But one cannot take the outcome for granted. Baldwin was not a politician and did not, I think, hope for politics to solve racism. Rather, his hope lay in reaching people's hearts with his words and by his example.

When *The Fire Next Time* was published, the book sold over a million copies and landed Baldwin on *Time* magazine's cover, which then was the imprimatur of notable accomplishment, success, and fame. Baldwin had become the emblem for betterment. The *Time* article accompanying the cover image noted,

> Not law, but morality is the basis of Baldwin's hopes. He says: "It is the responsibility of free men to trust and to celebrate what is constant—birth, struggle, and death are constant, and so is love—and to apprehend the nature of change, to be able and willing to change. I speak of change not on the surface but in the depths—change in the sense of renewal."[8]

I don't have sales figures for Baldwin's story collection *Going to Meet the Man*, which contained "Sonny's Blues," but across the sixty-five years since the story's first publication, it has been assigned and taught in secondary schools and in colleges and

[8] "Nation: The Root of the Negro Problem," *Time*, May 17, 1963, http://content.time.com/time/subscriber/article/0,33009,830326-1,00.html.

universities throughout the world, ultimately reaching many millions of readers. Both the essay and the story are famously known. They make illuminating companions when read in concert. Of the two, however, I would say that the story is the better known and has had the greatest impact. My sense of the story's power and its enduring influence comes from experiencing anew on each rereading the passion with which Baldwin summons me into the lives of Sonny and his brother. We are, after all, each other's keepers.

ACKNOWLEDGMENTS

This book would not exist without the inspiration of Anne Cheng, who suggested that I write it and who carefully and gracefully shepherded the work from first to last, offering guidance, suggestions, reassurance, humor, and affirmation all along the way. Carol Edgarian, my soul mate and my partner in all things, discussed, read, thought through, and contributed perspectives that I would have otherwise missed, adding her wisdom and heart from a lifetime of her own literary work, and gave me her steady encouragement. Mimi Kusch's keen eye and dedication to making sure that none of my errors of style, lapses of grammar and punctuation, and myriad misspellings went uncorrected would be essentially invisible in the book, unless noted here, because she always does her work so thoroughly and well. I'm also grateful to Jack McNichol and Aimee Wright at Oxford University Press for steering the project with knowing and confident hands. Finally, my appreciation goes out to the many writers and students whom I've been fortunate enough to read and work with across more than forty years—much of what I've learned and was able to offer in this book has resulted from the pleasure of conversations with all those others about the stories we share.

ABOUT THE AUTHOR

Tom Jenks is the cofounder and editor of *Narrative* Magazine (narrativemagazine.com). He is a former editor of *Esquire, Gentlemen's Quarterly,* and *The Paris Review,* and a senior editor at Scribner's, where he edited Hemingway's posthumous novel, *The Garden of Eden.* He has written for *Harper's, Ploughshares, Esquire, Vanity Fair, The American Scholar,* the *Los Angeles Times, Condé Nast Traveler,* the BBC, *Manhattan, Inc.,* the *Missouri Review, Columbia,* and elsewhere. Jenks has taught at the Iowa Writers' Workshop, the Creative Writing Programs at the University of California (Irvine and Davis), Washington University in St. Louis, the Squaw Valley and Bennington Summer Writing Workshops, and privately in New York, Boston, Washington DC, Chicago, Denver, Seattle, Portland, Los Angeles, and San Francisco. He can be found at tomjenks.com.

BIBLIOGRAPHY

Aristotle. *Poetics*. Translated by James Hutton. New York: Norton, 1982.

Auden, W. H. "Reading." *The Dyer's Hand*, 3–12. New York: Vintage, 1989.

Baldwin, James. *The Fire Next Time*. New York: Dell, 1962.

—. Baldwin, James. "Sonny's Blues." In *American Short Story Masterpieces*, edited by Raymond Carver and Tom Jenks, 1–32. New York: Dell, 1987.

—. Baldwin, James. "The Uses of the Blues." In *The Cross of Redemption: Uncollected Writings*, edited by Randall Kenan, 70–81. New York: Pantheon, 2010.

Campbell, James. *Talking at the Gates: A Life of James Baldwin*. Oakland: University of California Press, 1991.

Hughes, Langston. *The Weary Blues*. 1926. Reprint, New York: Dover, 2022.

Jones, Edward P. "All Aunt Hagar's Children." *The New Yorker*, December 22 and 29, 2003.

—. Jones, Edward P. "The Art of Fiction." *The Paris Review* 222, no. 207 (winter 2013). https://www.theparisreview.org/interviews/6283/the-art-of-fiction-no-222-edward-p-jones.

Kunitz, Stanley. "Action and Incantation." In *The Structure of Verse*, edited by Harvey Gross, 256, 258. New York: Ecco, 1966.

Lemming, David. *James Baldwin: A Biography*. New York: Arcade, 2015.

O'Connor, Flannery. *The Habit of Being: Letters of Flannery O'Connor*. Edited by Sally Fitzgerald. New York: Farrar, Straus & Giroux, 1979.

Ozick, Cynthia. *Metaphor & Memory*. New York: Vintage, 1980.

Porter, Lewis. *John Coltrane: His Life and Music*. Ann Arbor: University of Michigan Press, 2000.

Pritchett, V. S. *Chekhov: A Spirit Set Free*. New York: Random House, 1988.

Tolstoy, Leo. "What Is Art?" In *The Portable Tolstoy*, edited by John Bayley, 841–42. New York: Penguin, 1978.

Welty, Eudora. *The Optimist's Daughter*. New York: Vintage, 1969.

Welty, Eudora. *The Eye of the Story: Selected Essays and Reviews*. New York: Vintage, 1979.

Welty, Eudora. *One Writer's Beginnings*. Cambridge: Harvard University Press, 1984.

Woolf, Virginia. *A Room of One's Own*. New York: Harcourt, 1929.

INDEX

The manufacturer's authorised representative in the EU for product safety is Oxford University Press España S.A. of el Parque Empresarial San Fernando de Henares, Avenida de Castilla, 2 – 28830 Madrid (www.oup.es/en or product.safety@oup.com). OUP España S.A. also acts as importer into Spain of products made by the manufacturer.

www.ingramcontent.com/pod-product-compliance
Ingram Content Group UK Ltd.
Pitfield, Milton Keynes, MK11 3LW, UK
UKHW020656180726
473452UK00015B/141

* 9 7 8 0 1 9 2 8 8 4 2 6 8 *